Language Ideologies and Challenges of Multilingual Education in Ethiopia

The Case of Harari Region

Moges Yigezu

Organization for Social Science Research
in Eastern and Southern Africa (OSSREA)

©2010 Organisation for Social Science Research in Eastern and Southern Africa (OSSREA)

All rights reserved.

Printed in Ethiopia

ISBN: 978-99944-55-47-8

Copyeditors: *Matebu Tadesse*
              Abiye Daniel
Layout: *Alemtsehay Zewde*

Organisation for Social Science Research in
Eastern and Southern Africa (OSSREA)
P.O. Box 31971
Addis Ababa, Ethiopia
E-mail: ossrea@ethionet.et
Website: http//www.ossrea.net

OSSREA acknowledges the support of the Swedish International Development Co-operation Agency (Sida/SAREC), Norwegian Agency for Development Co-operation (NORAD), and The Netherlands' Ministry of Foreign Affairs.

TABLE OF CONTENTS

	Acknowledgements	iv
	Abbreviations	v
	Executive Summary	vi
Chapter One	Introduction	1
Chapter Two	Language Ideologies and Multilingualism in Education	11
Chapter Three	The History of Educational Language Policies in Ethiopia	23
Chapter Four	The Ethnography of Primary Schools in Harari: A Case Study	47
Chapter Five	Language Use, Attitudes and Patterns of Multilingualism	75
Chapter Six	Script Choice: Linguistic and Pedagogical Considerations	101
Chapter Seven	The Nature of the Curriculum	123
Chapter Eight	The Politics of Educational Language Planning	135
Chapter Nine	Summary, Conclusions and Recommendations	151
	References	156

ACKNOWLEDGEMENTS

I would like to extend my sincere gratitude to the Organization for Social Science Research in Eastern and Southern Africa (OSSREA) for financing this research. It is also my pleasure to express my appreciation to all who contributed to the development of this research in various ways. Particularly, I thank my research assistants, Tsion Issayas and Biniam Mitiku, for helping me in administering the questionnaires in the field and assisting me during the various interviews I have conducted. I am also grateful to my colleague Gideon Cohen for the insightful discussions we had on various topics; and to Fantahun Ayele and Tamire Andualem for their support and help in every possible way. I thank Debella Goshu for translating the questionnaires into Oromo and for assisting me by identifying materials related to Oromo orthography. Last but not least, my thanks to Orin Gensler for his very careful and critical reading of the manuscript, as regards both English and content.

ABBREVIATIONS

CSA	Central Statistics Authority
L1	first language (or mother tongue)
L2	second language (or language of wider communication)
L3	third language (international language)
LWC	language of wider communication
MT	mother tongue
MOI	medium of instruction
MTE	mother tongue education
SPSS	Statistical Package for the Social Sciences
SNNPR	Southern Nations Nationalities and Peoples Region

EXECUTIVE SUMMARY

During the last decade and a half, the use of local languages for official purposes, particularly in primary education, has become a pronounced characteristic of Ethiopian education system. The fact that as many as 22 languages have been introduced into the school system since mid 1990s represents a major ideological shift from the previous policies the country had adopted over the course of several centuries. The Ethiopian educational language policy is radical in its scope and unique in Sub-Saharan Africa and elsewhere, and it invites a close examination of its ideological foundation and, even more so, its implementation model.

In Ethiopia the language question is one of paramount importance, since the Constitution of 1995 confers rights up to secession to population groups on the basis of their ethno-linguisitc character. Ethiopia's geo-political units are thus primarily defined by language and ethnicity.

In this context, the ancient city of Harar presents a particularly interesting case for study and represents a unique geo-political entity within Ethiopia. The huge linguistic and related socio-political and ethnic diversities of Harar produce a microcosm of the Ethiopian State itself and thus provide a fertile ground for asking questions about multilingualism, federalism and ethnicity that have relevance beyond Harari Region itself.

The primary objective of this study was to make a critical appraisal of the implementation of vernacular education in the Harari region and examine the challenges of providing primary education in several Ethiopian and international languages, i.e. English, Amharic, Oromo, Arabic and Harari. The study made a comparative assessment of the use of languages as media of instruction for primary education, and concluded with an appraisal of the relative strengths and weaknesses in the use of each language, from both pedagogical and social perspectives.

The study has two major focal areas: policy formulation and policy implementation. The first part looked at the current educational language policy against the background of the socio-cultural history of the country and outlined the ideological foundations of this policy and its political and socio-economic implications. The second part examined the implementation model adopted and dealt with issues, such as the level of development of the languages involved in the school system, the school environment, the appropriateness of orthography, the teaching methods and materials used.

The research was a field study in which qualitative and quantitative primary data were gathered, classified, analyzed and interpreted using various techniques. Because of the multiple objectives outlined above, the study followed a mixed research method such that a qualitative research paradigm was be used for some parts of the research and a quantitative research paradigm for other parts. The two research paradigms are considered to be complementary in the sense that one set of results is complemented by another set of results and generalizations are made on findings that emerge from both methods together. The qualitative approach is used to carry out inquiry into the perceptions and aspirations of the community at the individual as well as the collective level. Types of qualitative research methods that have been employed to gather data include: historical survey, ethnographic research and phenomenological research.

The following conclusions have been drawn on the implementation of the policy of vernacular education in Harari.

It is clearly a multilingual education model, involving the use of three languages. Harari and Oromo are local mother tongues (L1) and Amharic is the indigenous language of wider communication (LWC) (L2). English and Arabic are foreign languages (L3). This model is in line with UNESCO's recommendation of having three languages (L1, L2 and L3) in multilingual primary education; a recommendation that follows from the position that teaching in the mother tongue is most effective in the academic achievement and cognitive development of the child. The model implemented in Harari has, therefore, a strong component of mother tongue education.

The model lacks a proper and consolidated policy towards the LWC, i.e. Amharic. The use of Amharic as a medium of instruction and the time allocation for the teaching of Amharic as a subject shows the highest disparity from school to school. Amharic, besides its political and psychological dominance, has a well developed literature which provides access to a much wider store of knowledge that can be provided by an indigenous language. Pupils who do not go beyond the first cycle will be cut off from the LWC and the accruing benefits that the knowledge of the language may provide. The drop-out rate for the region in the lower grades was between 18–23 per cent in the years 2000–2004. Since these children will have left school before mastering the LWC, which is the lingua franca of the region as well as the entire country, it will be very difficult for them to operate in other linguistic environments they are unfamiliar with. The need for the promotion of literacy in the LWC has not been adequately recognized by the political system of the region. This raises the question whether the policy is inherently unequal, denying equitable access to and achievement in basic education, and whether it respects the linguistic rights of the child. As rightly pointed out by Skutnabb-Kangas (2000), as much as a child has the right to learn in his/her mother tongue, he/she has the right to learn the official language of the country as a matter of linguistic right.

In terms of time allocation of each language within the classroom, a wide range of patterns has been observed between schools, even those using the same medium of instruction. The emphasis on one language or the other seems to depend on the interest of a particular school. This lack of consistency in language allocation in classrooms and the consequent disparity of competence in the major languages across pupils is another shortcoming of the implementation model.

The implementation model favours international languages over the official working language of the region and the country, Amharic. One of the shortcomings of the implementation model is, therefore, inadequate teaching of Amharic. Given the lack of uniformity in the teaching of the LWC the policy has no mechanism to ensure that disparities in mastering Amharic will be minimized, let alone eliminated.

In the area of language development and standardization of the vernaculars in use in the school system, there are persistent issues about which respondents have expressed their opinions. Lack of advance preparation on the part of the schools before the implementation of the policy, and inadequate involvement of the community in decision-making as well as in the implementation of the policy were concerns expressed by respondents. These facts have also been observed on the ground and are confirmed by interviews conducted with various stakeholders, such as teachers, school directors, policy-makers, and parents. Among the problems related to the implementation model and cited by the respondents, inconsistencies in the use of the orthography due to lack of standardization, variations in the pronunciation of some words, and lack of proper terminology for certain subjects are the major impediments.

In summary, then, the Harari Region, as compared to other Regional States, at least in its educational language policy, has an accommodative pluralist approach towards basic education by virtue of recognizing as many as five languages. The policy pursues an "official multilingualism" approach which provides an equitable amount of resources and attention to various groups. Hence, parents have the option to choose the school of their preference and exercise language rights on behalf of their children regardless of whether they are minors. This freedom of choice and opportunity has led to the wide range of implementation models. It cannot be expected that any single uniform implementation model could lead to satisfactory results in such a diverse multiethnic polity. A microcosm of Ethiopia cannot possibly operate with one uniform implementation model.

CHAPTER ONE
INTRODUCTION*

1.1. Background

Since 1991, Ethiopia has been a Federal State, comprised of Regional States that are organized on the basis of ethnicity and language. The use of regional and local languages for official purposes, particularly in primary education and the regional, zonal and district administrations, has become a pronounced characteristic of contemporary Ethiopian life. The introduction and use of regional and local languages are highly politicized, and often the practical implications are eclipsed by the political connotations of language use. Usually the use of local languages has been based on the political imperative to represent groups of people in the State, and not on perceived, or actual, benefits to pupils.

The language policy and the patterns of language use in Ethiopia thus provide an important locus for studying language ideology, particularly in connection with primary education. The fact that as many as 22 languages have been introduced into the school system during the last few decades, out of the 80 or so languages of the country, represents a major ideological shift from the previous policies the country has adopted over the course of several centuries. The policy, as it stands, is radical in its scope and unique in Sub-Saharan Africa and elsewhere and it invites a close examination of its ideological foundation and, even more so, its implementation model.

Important works have been carried out on language ideology within the African context and elsewhere (cf. Fardon & Furniss 1994; Bamgbose 1991; Srivastava 1984a; Khubchandani 1978). However, most of these works concern the use of colonial languages within post-colonial Africa. Ethiopia does not have a colonial past, except for a brief occupation by the Italians during the Second World War. English, nevertheless, plays an important role in Ethiopia because of its global importance, and its role in Ethiopian society continues to be crucial. Ethiopia, therefore, experiences various internal and external pressures related to language use both from within the country and resulting from the global situation.

The use of different scripts for Amharic and English and options regarding script and orthography in the realization of the written forms of other Ethiopian vernacular languages present additional challenges and necessitate sensitive language planning and policy development.

---

* The research reported on in this document was carried out in 2005-06. Changes since that time are unfortunately not covered.

Depending on the script selected for vernacular languages or languages of primary literacy, there is the possibility of using multiple scripts in a single geo-political unit. This further complicates the language use situation in Ethiopia and makes it a subject of both local and international importance.

The multilingual character of Ethiopia ensures that there are areas within a given geo-political unit where several languages are used by the population and where individuals are routinely able to use several languages. There is great flexibility in the use of languages in primary education, with schools in particular regions opting for the use of a language other than the official or regional language. Examples include the use of Amharic in urban areas in Oromiya Region and the use of Oromo in schools in the Oromo-speaking part of Wollo (Oromiya Zone of the Amhara Region), namely around Bati and Kemmissie. In Ethiopia, the language question is one of paramount significance, since the Constitution of 1995 (FDRE 1995) confers rights up to secession to population groups on the basis of their ethno-linguistic character. Ethiopia's geopolitical units are thus primarily defined by language and ethnicity. In this context, the ancient city of Harar presents a particularly interesting case for study and represents a unique geo-political entity within Ethiopia.

The Harari Region, with an area of 314 sq. km. (compare the largest region in Ethiopia, Oromiya: 335,422 sq. km.) and a population of 131,139 (CSA 1994) is one of the most diverse regions in Ethiopia in terms of ethnicity, language, religion, economic development and interethnic relationships. As such, it has been selected for this study because it enables us to understand the nature of multilingual and multiscriptual vernacular education and helps to address questions, such as: Why do people make particular decisions about language use in primary education? How do pupils learning in particular languages benefit or suffer as a result of these choices?

Politically, the Harari region is dominated by the Harari (Adere) ethnic group, who represent only seven per cent of the population (CSA 1994). The largest ethnic group is the Oromo, who account for 52 per cent of the population; the second largest ethnic group is the Amhara (37 per cent); the Somali ethnic group account for 1.7 per cent; other ethnic groups constitute 2.3 per cent (*ibid*). The most commonly spoken language is Amharic, which is employed as a mother tongue by ethnic Amharas and as lingua franca by all residents in the town and the vast majority of people in the rural areas of Harari Region.

Although the Amharic-speaking people, who comprise 37 per cent of the total population, have no official representation in the regional parliament, paradoxically the working official language of the regional government is Amharic. Amharic is a well-developed language with a rich literary tradition; politically coloured by its association with the Amhara ethnic group. The recognition of the Amharic language, but not of its speakers, thus reveals an interesting ideological stance regarding language and ethnicity within the wider context of ethnic federalism. Also other languages have great importance in the city. Among these, two international languages of wider communication, namely English and Arabic, are used in primary education. Somali is used by members of the Somali ethnic group as an unofficial language. Somali, Oromo, Amharic and Harari are all used in various aspects of commerce and trade. Amharic, Ge'ez and Arabic are mostly used for religious purposes.

Characterised by socio-linguistic history of competition among several dominant languages, Harari, also known as Adere, is culturally and historically dominant. It is an 'identity-preserving language' for the Harari ethnic group and has been also a written language since the 16th century. Amharic is societally and institutionally dominant. It is the language of wider communication (LWC) and the lingua franca of the people in the region. Oromo, on the other hand, has numerical and physical predominance as it has the majority of speakers in Harari Region and is also spoken as a regional language in the surrounding area. Ge'ez and Arabic, both languages of religion, which are affiliated to Christianity and Islam respectively, are mostly limited to uses for spiritual purposes, whereas English is globally dominant in the modern era. All these languages are vigorous competitors for linguistic dominance in Harari. This is what the "ecology of language" (see section 2.4) in the region looks like. The question is whether this ecology of language can create a mutually supportive system and produce equity.

The linguistic and the related socio-political and ethnic diversity is, therefore, so great as to produce a microcosm of the Ethiopian State itself and thus provides a fertile ground for asking questions about multilingualism, federalism and ethnicity that should have relevance beyond Harari Region itself.

Pedagogically, in primary education, five specified languages, namely *Harari, Oromo, Amharic, English* and *Arabic,* are currently employed as media of instruction and/or as a subject of study. Three scripts are used for these languages: (1) *Latin,* (2) *Ethiopic* and (3) *Arabic.* Amharic and Harari employ the Ethiopic script. English and Oromo use the Latin alphabet, albeit in different orthographic variations. In the Islamic Harari-, Oromo- and Somali-speaking communities, the Arabic script is used in Quranic schools as a language both of literacy and of religious study; and pupils thus have to achieve literacy in three writing systems at once.

This diversity in terms of ethnicity, language, and script is unmatched elsewhere in Ethiopia. The new education policy has been in effect in the Harari Region for over a decade. Switching between media of instruction in primary education entails a series of changes, and needs to be well-managed in order to attain maximum benefits from education. The use of a language that children already know as a medium of instruction is always a great advantage. However, as Baker (1993, 172) clearly states, "A recipe for success is unlikely to result from one ingredient (e.g. the language of the classroom)". Hence, if teachers lack proper materials, if there is no standardized spelling for the language, or if the orthography proposed has serious disadvantages because it is not based on a proper linguistic analysis of the sound system of the language, and if there are no pedagogical grammars to guide the teachers, nor any dictionaries or wordlists provided, the potential advantages of switching to the vernacular will be nullified (Baker 1996; Garcia 1998). Furthermore, if teachers are not trained to teach in the vernacular, and are not fully cognizant of the pedagogical opportunities it provides, or if they do not have sufficient respect for or understanding of the value of using the vernacular as the medium of instruction, this will also diminish the effectiveness of the use of the mother tongue as medium of instruction. It is, therefore, essential to study the situation in local schools to make sound judgments about the optimal uses of languages and the supporting factors which are necessary.

However, no study has assessed the implementation of the new education policy and impact of the introduction and use of multiple languages and scripts in the school system on provision of primary education in Harari. Cognizant of this gap, the researcher initiated this study.

1.2. Objectives of the Study

The primary objective of this work is, therefore, to make a critical appraisal of the implementation of vernacular education in the Harari Region and examine the challenges of providing primary education in several Ethiopian and international languages, i.e. English, Amharic, Oromo, Arabic and Harari. The study made a comparative assessment of the use of languages as media of instruction for primary education, and concluded with an appraisal of the relative strengths and weaknesses in the use of each language, from both pedagogical and social perspectives. It also investigated the challenges of multilingualism in terms of federalism, and how, in such city of a highly diverse language, economic development, ethnicity, and religion, one can produce equity in providing basic education for all. Finally, the study aimed to make recommendations concerning how to address the challenges of vernacular education in a multilingual and multiscriptual setting, such as Harar. The main goal of the project was to provide a knowledge base for the implementation of teaching programmes in the various languages that are used in Harari region.

More specifically, the study addresses the following two sets of issues: *language-oriented issues* and *learner-oriented issues.*

Language-oriented issues include: What would the variation of the languages of instruction look like in the school system? What is the level of standardization of each language? How is the choice of script made? What are the associated problems of transfer from mother tongues, such as Harari and Oromo, to Amharic, the national working language, and subsequently to English, which replaces all other languages as the official medium of instruction from grade seven up?

Learner-oriented questions included: How do pupils acquire reading skills, writing skills, comprehension skills, and analytical (interpretational) skills? What are the methods of teaching employed and how are these methods reflected in the teaching materials? What is the impact of the methods employed and how they are reflected in the teaching materials on the language proficiency of learners from minority groups, for whom the school language is not native language–as opposed to learners from majority groups, whose language is the medium of instruction and are, consequently, in an advantageous position from the outset?

1.3. Research Questions

The existence of a multitude of distinct linguistic groups within a geo-political entity raises complex questions for policy-makers, especially in developing countries. This study attempted to answer the following research questions.

- According to what criteria should languages be selected as media of instruction for use in primary education?
- What criteria should be employed to realize languages in a written form?
- In areas where, by necessity, more than one script is used, what mechanisms for combining and harmonizing the use of various languages and scripts can be developed in order to maximally facilitate the teaching/learning process?
- What are the pedagogical and linguistic considerations that should be taken into consideration in the preparation of teaching materials in various vernacular languages to be used in the primary schools?
- How does the attitude of the community towards the use of local languages and the choice of script affect the teaching/learning process?

1.4. Significance of the Study

The researcher believes this work has both academic and practical significances. The major practical and programmatic applications of the research will be to assist in the planning process in the continued development and use of international and vernacular languages in primary education in Harari Region. It will also be useful in attempts to examine the Region as a linguistic entity. The example provided by Harar will also be of significance in providing a microcosm for looking at language ideologies and the application of language policy and planning processes in Ethiopia as a whole. The academic significance of the study is that it provides a case study within the broader international debate on language ideologies surrounding the development of language policies and language planning.

1.5. Research Methodology

1.5.1. The Study Design

The research was a field study, in which qualitative and quantitative primary data were gathered, described, classified, analyzed, and interpreted using various techniques. Because of the study aimed at multiple objectives, it followed a mixed research method such that a qualitative method was used for some parts of the research and a quantitative method for other parts. The qualitative and quantitative methods were used in a sense that results obtained using one method were complemented by another set of results obtained using the other method and then generalizations were made based on findings that emerged from both methods together.

The qualitative approach was used to inquire into the perceptions and aspirations of the community at individual as well as collective levels. The qualitative methods that were employed to gather data include the following:

(1) Historical survey: a survey of the history of educational language policies was made by consulting archives and historical sources in order to appraise the historical basis of Ethiopian language policies and their ideological foundations.

(2) Ethnographic research: An ethnographic study of selected schools was made in order to see the educational practices in the schools by describing the type of the schools, background of pupils, languages used in the school system, entry or exit levels for each language, orthographies used, time allocated to teach each language, and the nature of the classroom. The knowledge-based resource to be developed to provide knowledge base for the implementation of teaching programmes in the various languages that are used in Harari region will have mainly linguistic aspect. In order to ensure that this knowledge will be of the type that is most useful to school programmes, and that it can be used effectively in the development of new teaching materials and teaching practices, ethnographic studies of the local schools in the region were included.

(3) Phenomenological research: in order to generate qualitative data of both a social and a linguistic nature, participant observation, focus group discussions and interviewing key informants, including pupils, teachers, parents and educationalists or authorities in the Regional Bureau of Education, were used. These methods jointly provide a useful way to study the attitudes of pupils, parents, teachers and educationalists in the Regional Bureau of Education on language and script choices as well as on the use of vernaculars for primary education. Focus group discussions (one for each school, and six to eight people in each group) were conducted between the researcher and

respondents (education experts, textbook designers, etc.) in order to validate the information collected in the interviews.

Supplementary quantitative approach was employed during fieldwork conducted in the city of Harar and surrounding rural areas. This involved a sociolinguistic survey using three sets of questionnaires to gather information on patterns of language use and attitudes as well as patterns of multilingualism.

1.5.2. The Study Area

The six schools selected were the following (see the details on the ethnography of the schools in Chapter Four):

- A religious-oriented school where the medium of instruction for all secular subjects is Harari, and Arabic is used for religious study;
- A government school where Harari is used as medium of instruction;
- A government school where Amharic is the medium of instruction;
- An international school where English and Amharic are media of instruction, i.e. a dual-language approach; and
- Two schools in which Oromo is the medium of instruction, one from an urban and another from a rural area.

The schools were selected based on various parameters: the type of school, the language used as medium of instruction, and where applicable, a rural vs. urban dichotomy. Amharic, Harari and English are used as media of instruction only in urban areas while Oromo is used in both urban and rural areas. In fact, in all rural areas the medium of instruction is only Oromo since the majority of the population are native Oromo speakers. Arabic is given as a subject only in religious-oriented schools in the city of Harar as a language of literacy and religious study.

1.5.3. Sampling

The sampling covered a variety of schools that use different languages as medium of instruction. Based on the type of school, the language used as medium of instruction, and where applicable, a rural vs. urban dichotomy, six schools were chosen to represent the four languages (Amharic, Harari, English, and Oromo) that are used as media of instruction. After selecting the schools, the population was stratified into different categories, such as male and female, teachers and pupils, government officials, and civil servants. A random sample was taken from each of these stratified groupings. The sampling procedure was meant to enable ensure that each of the stratified population groups would have an equal chance to be interviewed.

In each school, sample pupils of grade 4, 5 and 6 were interviewed. The pupils were selected by random sampling. A total of 678 pupils, 222 parents and 87 teachers were randomly selected. The sample size for the study covering the six schools was therefore a total of 987 respondents. In addition, 22 community leaders, school directors, educational authorities and civil servants were interviewed and participated in the focus group discussions.

1.5.4. Data Collection and Analysis

Qualitative data were gathered through historical survey, ethnographic research, and phenomenological research that involved participant observation, focus group discussions and interviewing key informants.

Supplementary quantitative data were gathered during field work in the city of Harar and surrounding rural areas through a sociolinguistic survey, which involved the use of three sets of questionnaires. To obtain primary data, the researcher and assistants administered the questionnaires to sample pupils, parents, and teachers in the six schools. The questionnaires included questions related to the respondent's background information, patterns of language use, and attitude referring to language and script choice as well as patterns of multilingualism. Unlike self-administered questionnaires, interviews provide insight into in-depth information and feelings, which help to get "inside" information by learning from non-verbal messages from respondents. The objective was to explore "what is happening" by using some guided questions to probe for deep information and knowledge. The data generated from the questionnaires were processed using SPSS software, and were analyzed by using descriptive statistical methods, such as the computation of sample means, medians, or modes.

1.6. Organisation of the Study

The study has two major focal areas/parts: 1) policy formulation, and 2) policy implementation. The first part comprises Chapters 1–3 and looks at the current educational language policy against the background of the socio-cultural history of the country and outlines the ideological foundations of this policy and its political and socio-economic implications. The second part examines the implementation model adopted and deals with issues, such as the level of development of the languages involved in the school system, the school environment, the appropriateness of orthography, the teaching methods and materials used.

Chapter one gives the background of the study, the objectives of the study, statement of the problem, major research questions, significance and limitations of the study, the methodology employed, and data collection procedures. The second chapter provides a critical review of related literature and presents the conceptual frameworks adopted to explain the various issues pertaining to language ideologies and linguistic rights. It also discusses the concept of 'linguistic ecology' and its impact on one of the most diverse regions of Ethiopia, and looks into the concept of equity in a multilingual educational system. Furthermore, this chapter deals with the idea of 'language transfer' and its importance in the teaching/learning process. The third chapter sketches the history of educational language policy in Ethiopia and discusses the varying ideological outlooks reflected in the political systems of successive regimes of Ethiopia, including the present one.

The second part of the study has four chapters (Chapters 4–7). Chapter four describes the ethnography of schools in Harari region as manifested in selected representative schools. It gives insight into the school environment and educational practices, describing the types of schools, the languages used in the school system, the language allocation in classroom, the entry and exit level of each language used in the school, and the manner of classroom management. The fifth chapter is devoted to the quantitative analysis of data to assess the attitude of pupils, parents and teachers towards language and script choices and the use of vernaculars in primary education. This chapter presents results of investigation of learner-oriented issues from both linguistic and pedagogical perspectives, dealing with language use and patterns of multilingualism, language attitudes and choices in relation to the concepts of 'preference', 'opportunity', and 'identity'. The sixth chapter tackles the issue of script choice, looks into the effect of using multiple scripts in the school system, and explores the origin and nature of each script currently in use. It also discusses conditions, constraints and political imperatives that have affected and influenced script choice, and looks into how pupils can benefit or suffer as a result of these choices. Chapter seven highlights the level of standardization of the languages employed as media of instruction, the development of teaching materials in these languages, the method of teaching reflected in these materials, and the idea of transfer or bridging between the various languages involved in the teaching/learning process.

Finally, Chapter eight presents problems and challenges of giving basic education in an equitable manner in multiple languages and scripts and examines the practical, theoretical and policy issues in a multilingual setting, such as Harari and beyond. The last chapter summarizes the findings of the study and presents recommendations for policy makers and educationalists concerning how best to address the challenges of a multilingual and multiscriptual vernacular education system.

CHAPTER TWO

LANGUAGE IDEOLOGIES AND MULTILINGUALISM IN EDUCATION

2.1. Language Ideologies

A language ideology can be broadly defined as a set of beliefs and attitudes about language, language use and language practices. According to Spolsky (2004, 14), language ideologies "designate a speech community's consensus on what value to apply to each of the language variables". Schiffman (1996, 5) refers to language ideologies as "linguistic culture", which encompasses "the set of behaviours, assumptions, cultural forms, prejudices, folk belief systems, attitudes, stereotypes, ways of thinking about language, and religio-historical circumstances associated with a particular language".

The concept of language ideology links language issues to the social, psychological and moral interests of the speakers. Woolard & Schieffelin, commenting on the relevance of the study of language ideologies as an important scholarly inquiry state, "Ideologies of language are significant for social as well as linguistic analysis because they are not only about language. Rather, such ideologies envision and enact links of language to group and personal identity, to aesthetics, to morality, and to epistemology" (1994, 55–56). "Not only linguistic forms but social institutions such as the nation-state, schooling, gender, dispute settlement, and law hinge on the ideologization of language use" (*ibid*).

Within the context of a multilingual and multiscriptual vernacular education system, such as in Harar, distinct ideological assumptions are reflected in the choice of languages, the role languages play in the curriculum, and the level at which each language is introduced. The ideological stances towards vernacular languages, the language of wider communication, Amharic, and the international languages, English and Arabic, have been entrenched in the implementation models which the schools have adopted with the aim of providing basic primary education in an equitable manner in multiple languages (see details in Chapter Four).

In a society where many languages are unwritten, or in a situation where multiple scripts are in use, any particular form of graphic representation can be contested and orthographic battles may ignite. This is an instance where language ideologies transparently influence and affect the implementation of a policy since "orthographic systems cannot be conceptualized simply as reducing speech to writing, but rather they are symbols that carry historical, cultural, and political meanings" (Woolard & Schieffelin 1994, 65). The Harari language in this particular case provides a classic example as its written tradition, which goes back to the 16th century, has passed through complex orthographic developments, adopting different scripts—Arabic, Latin and Ethiopic, at different times in its history. The change of scripts can be attributed to shifts in ideological outlooks. The orthographic reform in Harari is still going on and has not been settled yet (see Section 6.6).

The idea of standardizing and developing the vernaculars for modern use, such as for education, is more of an ideological process than merely a linguistic fact, as it involves doctrines of 'correctness' and 'purism'. The idea of purism is closely related to the ideology of linguistic assimilation, and brings about similar results. It can be best described in terms of feelings and attitudes towards an ideal form of a language, usually in its written state (Daoust 1997, 443).

The use of multiple languages and scripts in a multiethnic and multilingual setting, such as Harar thus demands several delicate decisions at different stages of planning and implementation of policy. These decisions are ideologically grounded and historically contingent; and are, therefore, shaped by political, social and economic factors.

Language ideologies very often derive from the political philosophy of the power structure in which the country's national ideals are constructed. The vision and mission of the political system, described in the preamble of the nation's constitution, reflect the type of ideology the system follows regarding language and language use. In other words, the national ideals stated by the political system mirror the kind of socio-political framework the country has adopted, which in turn affects the official language use pattern and the language planning strategies. In Ethiopia, the guiding political philosophy today is "ethnic federalism", which takes language and ethnicity as the main variables in delimiting the country's geopolitical structure.

Research on language ideologies and the role of languages in society recognizes a taxonomy of language ideologies underlying language planning efforts: *assimilation, pluralism, vernacularization* and *internationalization* (Cobarrubias 1983). These ideological stances correspond to deep-seated orientations that view language as a resource, a problem or as the linguistic right of the individual (Bamgbose 1991, 1994; Baker 1996, 353–359; Ruiz 1984).

Assimilation and pluralism are two extreme ideological positions. The ideology of assimilation asserts that cultural groups should give up their heritage cultures and adopt the dominant society's way of life, a view captured in the idea of 'melting pot'. The concept of 'a melting pot' has two varieties. One is a situation where all cultural groups melt together until the final product is a unique combination. The other is a situation where cultural groups are expected to conform to the dominant national culture. The opposite view, pluralism, advocates that cultural groups should maintain their heritage culture as much as possible.

The assimilationist ideology conceives linguistic diversity as a source of political problems connected to national or regional disunity and inter-group conflict. According to this outlook, linguistic diversity may harm integration and social cohesiveness, and create more antagonism and conflict in society. These perceived problems regarding linguistic diversity are to be resolved by assimilation of minority languages into a majority language. The aim here is to achieve monolingualism as a strategy for avoiding the perceived complications allegedly resulting from diversity of languages.

Opponents of this view argue that the use of two or more languages is rarely the cause of tension, disunity, conflict and discord; and hence advocate pluralism as opposed to assimilation. They further argue that linguistic diversity and national unity can co-exist as in, for example, Singapore, Luxembourg, or Switzerland (Baker 1996,353); conversely, the use of a single language neither guarantees national unity nor secures peace and stability, as witnessed in the recent history of Somalia, a linguistically homogenous country. The history of war there shows that, rather than linguistic diversity, economic, political and religious differences are prominent causes of conflict. Languages are very often used as a proxy in order to advance other economic and political conflicts because "ideologies that appear to be about language, when carefully reread, are revealed to be coded stories about political, religious, or scientific conflicts..." (Gal 1998, 323).

In the context of multilingual education, various types of assimilation may occur in a given polity and assimilation may also be explicit, implied or concealed (Tosi 1988 as quoted in Baker 1996, 365). According to this view, explicit assimilation occurs when language minority children are required to take monolingual education solely in the majority language. Implied assimilation takes place when such children are diagnosed as having 'special needs' and are offered compensatory forms of education, i.e. providing transitional bilingual education when children do not speak the dominant language. Concealed assimilation may be found in some types of multicultural education programmes where language minorities may be instructed in racial harmony, national unity, and individual achievement using majority language criteria to measure success in order to achieve hegemony and ethnic harmony (*ibid*).

Ideologies embodying the notions of 'integration', 'pluralism' and 'multiculturalism' have challenged the assimilationist philosophy, as Baker (1996, 366) points out. The picture of the melting pot is contrasted with alternative images: *the tossed salad, the linguistic mosaic* and *the language garden*. This opposite view, pluralism or integration, has been described by a popular metaphor *the salad bowl*, with the ingredients separate and distinguishable, but contributing in a valuable and unique way to the whole. Another integration metaphor, favoured in Canada, is the *linguistic mosaic*, with different pieces joined together in one holistic arrangement (*ibid*).

The use of one's language is also viewed as a basic human right, in that there should be an individual right to the choice of language just as there is an individual right to the choice of religion. Adherents of this view argue that such linguistic rights are derived from personal rights, i.e. the right to freedom of expression (Baker 1996, 354). Trueba quoted in Baker (1996, 357), asserts, "Language rights of ethno-linguistic minorities are not detachable from their basic human rights, their rights to their culture and their civil rights" (Trueba 1991, 44). Such rights may also be derived from international declarations made by organizations like UNESCO, EU, etc. Yet another source from which linguistic rights may be derived is through constitutional rights codified in the legal system. The argument here stresses that linguistic diversity should be celebrated.

Along the same line of argument, linguistic diversity or multilingualism is viewed as a resource at both personal and national levels. The ideology of 'language as a resource' considers minority languages in particular "as a cultural and social resource" (Baker 1996, 357). Baker further argues that "While languages may be viewed in terms of their economic bridge building potential, languages may also be supported for their ability to build social bridges across different groups, bridges for cross fertilization between cultures".

In parallel to 'pluralism' and 'assimilation' the other two ideological outlooks, 'vernacularization' and 'internationalism', similarly rest on opposing assumptions. Vernacularization is an ideology that supports the recognition, promotion and development of minority languages alongside the international language and/or the language of wider communication. It involves, among other things, designing orthographies for unwritten languages, standardizing a variety of a language for modern use, and introducing minority languages into the school system for primary education. Daoust (1997, 445) notes that vernacularization at times involves the restoration of a literary language as the case of classical Arabic in North Africa (Tunisia and Algeria), where classical Arabic was recognized as an official language in lieu of French, and the extreme case of vernacularization is the revival of Hebrew in Israel.

Internationalism, on the other hand, is an ideology that advocates the adoption of an international language as a nation's official language. Very often, this view is motivated by political reasons and argues that the use of an international language facilitates socio-economic and cultural advancement by giving access to science and technology (*ibid*). This is basically a nationalist ideology that promotes assimilation and views linguistic diversity as a problem to social and economic advancement.

Hence, the equation of language and nation, the quest for the recognition of cultural pluralism or linguistic diversity, the notion of preservation of cultural heritage, and the advocacy of any form of globalization are attitudes and beliefs that rely on and reinforce an ideological conception of language.

2.2. Multilingualism in Education

Multilingual education has been recommended in multilingual societies as a result of studies over several decades, for both pedagogical and ideological reasons. However, worldwide most primary education systems in multilingual societies continue to be monolingual, functioning either in the language of the elite or in a language of wider communication. Over the last few decades, several case studies focusing on vernacular education and multilingual language policies have been produced.

Fardon & Furniss (1994), in *African Languages, Development and the State,* and Bamgbose (1991), in *Language and the Nation,* discuss critically the prevalent idea that linguistic diversity represents a problem that African states must address. Both works challenge this view and present the alternative argument that linguistic diversity is a resource upon which human and material development can and should be based. Bamgbose argues for the development of multilingual education systems that allow a role for local or regional languages within the primary education system. His arguments rely on the pedagogical and psychological advantages that mother tongue education offers to children. Both works, moreover, focus on the importance of including citizens within state structures through the use of their mother tongues in order to avoid fragmentation and marginalization. The authors further argue that social dislocation of marginalized groups inevitably presents political problems for the state, which the use of regional languages may help to avoid or resolve.

Eastman (1983) and Cooper (1989) argue that language planning and development must reflect and support the existing desires and aspirations of the population. Eastman asserts the fundamental importance of basing language planning upon research into attitudes. She also explains that language planning cannot be successful in the absence of adequate material support, even if the policy is well designed. Cooper asserts that language planning is, in itself, a statement about direction in which the society itself is expected to develop, highlighting the ideological framework adopted by the government. He argues that planning language use is identical with planning the nature of society. Along the same line of argument, McNabb (1989) stresses the importance of continuing research into attitudes as a major basis for the development of language policy.

Brenzinger (1997) discusses the importance of developing solutions to language diversity based on multilingual ideologies. He asserts the need to develop multiple solutions to the problem of language use in primary education. Cohen (2000) argues that the different conditions in urban and rural areas, and between different language groups, require locally specific solutions that must balance local attitudes and desires, practical realities and the need to satisfy national objectives. This process is inevitably complex and gaps between policy and practice should be acknowledged and addressed as part of efforts to secure better application of language planning. Gfeller (1998) and (1999) looks at the use of local languages in primary education along with maintaining the use of the official language, Amharic, in the Southern Region of Ethiopia and argues in favour of multilingual education as the most appropriate model for Africa and beyond in the age of globalization.

Within the Ethiopian educational system, primary education is generally defined as the completion of the first cycle, i.e. grade 1–4, during which period children should be transformed from illiterate to literate, and should develop the basic skills of reading and writing. An important issue in a multilingual setting is the choice of the medium through which primary education is to be achieved. In a multiethnic society, such as Harar, choices regarding multilingual education are determined by various interrelated factors ranging from social, historical, ideological, and psychological aspects to power-relations between the parties involved. All these factors should be considered in deciding the medium through which primary education will be provided.

There are two opposing claims on the issue of the medium of primary education: (1) primary education is most effectively achieved in the mother tongue (cf. UNESCO 1953), and (2) it is most effectively achieved in the language of wider communication, i.e. the official language or an international language. These two claims result in different planning choices with regard to the language of primary education. The first claim, in its extreme form, leads to a curriculum exclusively in the mother tongue and can be labelled as "pluralist" in its orientation, while the second claim, in its most extreme form, leads to a monolingual curriculum generally in an official language, and is usually termed "assimilationist".

Yet another option advocates for a situation in which literacy is first introduced in the child's mother tongue, and once the basic literacy skills are attained, the curriculum transfers to a formal or official language of education. In other words, primary education is taught through the child's mother tongue and then education continues through the exogenous official language. This model is known as "vernacular-cum-transfer literacy" and has been applied in many countries, such as India (Srivastava 1984b). This is roughly the kind of model that is currently in effect in the Ethiopian educational system in general and in the Harari region in particular. Whether this switch from the vernacular to the official language is well planned and proceeds smoothly in a multilingual education programme remains to be seen in the course of this research.

2.3. Language Transfer and Cognitive Development

The nature of multilingual vernacular education has been the subject matter of various disciplines such as educational science and linguistics. In educational science, the positive effects of multilingualism have been recognized for some time (Jebner 1997, 17), whereas in linguistics scholars examining second language acquisition have differing views on the nature of multilingualism and its effects on individuals' cognitive development.

One of these views adopts the Chomskyan paradigm, which is based on a homogenous competence model, whereby a bilingual is believed to have two separate language competences and is essentially considered as the sum of two monolinguals in one person. This model suggests the existence of two independent psychological mechanisms—one for each language. In this model variation is seen as a feature of performance rather than a reflection of the learner's underlying knowledge system. In contrast, the psycholinguistic model asserts that a bilingual person is not the sum of two monolinguals but has a specific linguistic configuration characterized by the constant interaction and coexistence of the two languages involved (*ibid*). This model is known as the "interdependency hypothesis" and assumes that there are two separate but interrelated psycholinguistic mechanisms in the mind of the bilingual. It also identifies positive cognitive consequences of bilingualism and argues "bilingual children show definite advantages on measures of metalinguistic awareness, cognitive flexibility and creativity or divergent thought" (Jebner 1977, 20).

Complex multilingual settings in primary education, such as that found in Harar, necessitate a consideration of issues including the level of language proficiency and cognitive development of individual children. Most studies on multilingual language acquisition have been carried out in highly literate environments, such as the USA, Canada, and Europe. How far their findings can be applied to situations where literate communication does not apply for the larger section of the population has not been adequately discussed. Bearing in mind these limitations, this study followed a psycholinguistic model of multilingual proficiency developed in theories of second language acquisition, namely the "interdependency hypothesis" as developed by Cummins (1979) and the systematic exploitation of "potential transfer" between languages and subjects (Sharwood Smith 1994) that have been argued to be effective in learning a second language.

The 'interdependency hypothesis' asserts that there is a certain degree of interdependence between the first language or mother tongue and second language in the development of the cognitive skills of an individual child. Alternatively stated, the bilingual child is not simply the sum of two monolinguals but develops specific psycholinguistic mechanisms in which both languages interact to various degrees (Hamers & Blanc 1989, 214). The proficiency in second language is, therefore, at least partially dependent on the level to which the first language has been developed. This observation has led to the assumption that a distinction has to be made between 'surface fluency' and a more cognitively demanding and academically related language proficiency (Gfeller 1998, 195). Academic achievement requires a deeper knowledge of the language, or so-called 'cognitive-academic language proficiency'. Surface fluency may enable the speaker to engage in face-to-face conversations but depends heavily on contextual cues, which typically are very limited or totally missing in classroom situations. The pupil's language proficiency in a multilingual programme thus allows making use of what Cummins (1979) calls the 'common underlying proficiency', i.e. a multilingual pupil will integrate input from all languages he or she knows well to form a common integrated knowledge base. The language skills that pupils have acquired in one language are used in any other language they may have learnt all the way up to the level of 'cognitive-academic language proficiency'. The interdependency hypothesis, therefore, gives a theoretical basis for looking at the transfer potential in multilingual education.

2.3.1. Negative Transfer

Contrastive Analysis (negative transfer) and the Creative Construction Hypothesis (positive transfer) are two ways of dealing with second language acquisition. Contrastive analysis is founded on the assumption that language learning is the formation of a set of habits, and an established set of habits in the first language either facilitates or impedes the establishment of a new set of habits in second language learning. It is assumed that by comparing the features of the two languages, difficulties of the language learner can be predicted in situations where speakers tend to use the forms of their first language and apply them in the second language system. This assumption prompts the notions of 'transfer' and 'interference' whereby previous knowledge of the first language is used to facilitate the learning of a second language.

2.3.2. Positive Transfer

The Creative Construction Hypothesis, on the other hand, is based on assumed similarities between first and second language acquisitions and asserts that there are certain general universal language acquisition rules which the child acquires in his first language and which will be re-applied in any subsequent second language acquisition.

The potential transfer in the case of Harari Region will take place between linguistically unrelated or distantly related languages and between scripts of different natures. Potential transfer between the scripts employed may involve both positive and negative transfer features between the alphabetic writing system (signs represent either consonants or vowels) and the syllabic writing system (each sign represents a vowel/consonant combination). There are also differences in direction of writing; Ethiopic and Latin are written from left to right whereas Arabic is written from right to left. On the other hand, potential transfer between languages will involve the basic learning principles developed in second language acquisition research. These include: the learner builds his knowledge (both linguistic and general) in constant interaction with his environment; comparison is employed as a major strategy in understanding new information; a certain level of linguistic proficiency in the classroom language is necessary to make the teaching-learning process fruitful; and literacy acquisition draws heavily on previous knowledge of language and the immediate environment (Gfeller 1998). It must be stressed that "Language transfer is best thought of as a cover term for the whole class of behaviours, processes and constraints, each of which has to do with cross linguistic influence, i.e. the influence and use of prior knowledge, usually but not exclusively native language knowledge" (Selinker 1992, 208 cited in Gfeller 1998).

2.4. The Concept of "Linguistic Ecology"

The concept of linguistic ecology has been effectively utilized by some linguists, such as Haugen (1971), Muhlhausler (1997), and Spolsky (2004) as a tool to capture the complex relationships between languages, their speakers and the environment or the cultural context in which they are being used. Haugen (1971), as quoted in Spolsky (2004, 7), defines linguistic ecology as, "the study of the interactions between any given language and its environment". In this ecological model, linguistic ecology begins with a particular geographical area, not with a particular language, and it is not the size or number of languages that matters but the meaningful relationships that exist between the languages, the users and the cultural system in which the languages and the users are operating.

Muhlhausler (1997, 4—5), in his insightful discussion of the relationship between language ecology and conflict, outlines the salient features that characterize linguistic ecology: (1) it is inhabited by a diversity of inhabitants, (2) the relationship between the inhabitants is dynamic and changing, (3) it is sustained by functional links between its inhabitants, (4) it is not the absolute number of diverse inhabitants but the links between them which are important, (5) lack of such links leads to conflict and potential collapse, and (6) the links create a mutually supportive system. He defines linguistic ecology as, "a dynamic system consisting of a number of inhabitants and meaningful interconnections between them" and further argues that languages (not speakers) should be considered as the inhabitants, with other parameters, such as the speaker's situation as the supporting habitat.

The idea of linguistic ecology has been linked to issues, such as language contact, social conflict and conflict reduction. As suggested in the outlined salient features of linguistic ecology, the absence of sustained meaningful links between the inhabitants may lead to social conflict or disaster; which implies that language contact may potentially involve social conflict. Muhlhausler (1997, 6), nonetheless, cites two possible positive scenarios across languages and cultures: (1) some cases where languages with only a few speakers have survived in an environment where many larger surrounding languages are spoken; and (2) other cases where a dozen or so languages coexist in a very compact geographical area for centuries in conditions of constant contact. Muhlhausler concludes that language contact need not necessarily involve conflict since "social conflict and language contact are independent parameters, not part of the same package and that unity and cooperation are compatible with both a high degree of linguistic diversity and contact as well as quasi-monolingualism and isolation".

Harlech-Jones (1997, 244) quoting Rawls (1973, 62) states that conflicts that are seemingly about languages are in fact about the "chief primary goods at the disposition of society", which are "rights and liberties, powers and opportunities, income and wealth". He further contends that language conflict "is a conflict in which language has become a focus of contention because it is seen as enhancing or inhibiting access to these 'primary goods' ".

A healthy linguistic ecology could also further conflict reduction. Muhlhausler points out that 'stable multilingualism' and 'intercultural settings' are the main factors fostering conflict reduction, and the two functional types of languages required for conflict reduction are 'identity preserving languages' and 'linking languages' or lingua franca. When these are absent, then conflict may arise. For instance, colonial practices, conquest, displacements and an ill-conceived policy can be ecologically disruptive.

In Harari, as pointed out in the foregoing discussions, there are three major languages in competition, namely Harari, Oromo and Amharic. The competition is politically motivated and is primarily between Oromo and Harari, the two vernaculars. A recent case study on the political inclusion and exclusion of non-Harari ethnic groups in the region reveals, "Some of the major causes of conflict are competition for resources and political marginalization" (Yared 2005, 47). The root cause of ethnic conflict, according to Yared (2005), is the exclusionist nature of the political arrangement in the region and the consequent political marginalization of non-Harari groups. Among the non-Harari groups, the Oromo are numerically dominant; the Amhara are historically and psychologically dominant, but they are numerically second to the Oromo and they have no place in the regional political arrangement.

Functionally, while Harari and Oromo are identity-preserving languages, Amharic is the linking language or the lingua franca and the official working language of the regional government. All three of the competing languages are used as media of instruction in schools at the primary level. Other important languages are Arabic associated with Islam, the dominant religion in the region, and English considered as the language of higher education. There is a functional relationship between each language and the cultural environment in which the language is operating. The question is whether the current functional links among the inhabitants (languages) and the cultural environment will tend to create a mutually supportive system or lead to potential conflict.

2.5. Equity in a Multilingual Education System

The prime objective of the Ethiopian educational reform of 1994 was to provide equal opportunity to all children of school age by ensuring free and compulsory primary education of good quality. The concern often expressed, however, is about what may be called "educational delivery".

That is, do all children have equal access to social and economic opportunities through learning in the mother tongue? In an evaluative account of the Ethiopian education reform and its implementation in the Southern Nations Nationalities and Peoples Region of Ethiopia, Pursley (1997, 8) observes, "Equity problems persist since the level of development of Ethiopian languages is uneven and support and supplementary materials are much richer in some languages than in others". Also Cohen (2005) argues that equity may be compromised by the use of multiple languages for two reasons. First, the different level of development of different languages affects their usefulness as languages of education, which in turn affects the quality of education that schools are able to provide. Second, differences in overall patterns of language use mean that different languages do not in fact provide equal opportunities.

In Harari region, for example, the school year in which Amharic is introduced into the curriculum varies from one school to another, and the lack of a mechanism to compensate for the disparities in mastering the official language of the region and the nation may have the effect of denying equitable access to opportunities. On the other hand, parents' freedom of choice in sending their children to schools of their preference might contribute positively to producing equity. In a situation where languages have different levels of standardization and development as well as different patterns of usage, the concept of equity provides an important theoretical frame within which to consider the use of languages. Language policy and its model of implementation, as part of the overall political and social policy, may, therefore, serve to enhance or inhibit access to equal opportunities and equitable distribution of the intellectual goods of society. In light of this, in the forthcoming chapters, we shall examine whether the use of vernaculars in the schools has empowered minority groups and produced equity as envisaged in the education reform of 1994.

In summary, the aforementioned conceptual frameworks have been briefly surveyed here to make possible a comprehensive analysis of this multifaceted and complex field. First, we have outlined the language beliefs or ideologies affecting and influencing language diversity and the values and prestige speakers assign to their language, as part of a speech community's consensus, and the foundations of those beliefs and ideologies. Second, the concept of "language transfer" has been discussed in order to see how the switch from the vernacular to the official language is conducted and how this process affects the teaching and learning process. Language transfer is also important in the context of the psycholinguistic theory of language acquisition that enables us to describe and explain the transfer potential from one language to another and from one type of script to another. Third, the concept of "linguistic ecology" has been introduced as a useful framework to describe the complex relationships of any given language and its environment. By employing an ecological approach, an attempt was made to determine the functional link between the languages and their cultural environment. Finally, the idea of "equity" has been brought into focus, as an important theoretical frame within which to consider language use in a multilingual setting. These multiple conceptual frameworks proved to be complementary in explaining issues pertaining to providing vernacular education in multiple languages and scripts in the highly diverse and geographically compact setting of Harar, and in other contexts as well.

CHAPTER THREE

THE HISTORY OF EDUCATIONAL LANGUAGE POLICIES IN ETHIOPIA

3.1. Introduction

Educational language policies can only be properly understood when related to the philosophy and ideology held by the political system and the politics connected to the society. The decisions made about issues, such as which language to use in basic education, when and how to teach the vernacular, how to manage a multilingual classroom, what type of curriculum material to be adopted, and what type of script to be adopted are not only based on pedagogical imperatives. At the societal and government levels, these decisions are influenced and dictated by the ideology of the political system. At the level of the classroom and school environment, the practices are surrounded and underpinned by a set of beliefs and attitudes about languages and language use. Educational language policies are, therefore, directly or indirectly, interwoven into politics and grounded in the ideology and power structure of the nation and the society at large.

Historically, Ethiopia diverges from the other Sub-Saharan African states and hence the history of Ethiopian education has two distinct features: (1) it has a tradition of writing that is centuries old and which has been in use in the church and in the cultural, educational and state affairs of the country since the time of the Axum civilization; (2) it does not have a colonial past, except for a brief occupation by the Italians during the Second World War. Ethiopia also has a long tradition of using an indigenous language in its formal education and as a national-official language, as well as a lingua franca.

Over the course of several centuries, the governments of Ethiopia have adopted language and educational policies, which were ingrained in the then-dominant ideologies, and aimed to govern and 'modernize' the nation. The policies were profoundly moulded by the social, political, and cultural past of the country. Pankhurst (1976, 305), in his description of the history of education in Ethiopia, notes that the educational system of the country "owes much of its distinctive character to the fact that Ethiopia is the only African country to have both remained predominantly Christian for over a millennium and a half, and to have preserved its ancient independence throughout the European 'Scramble for Africa'". There was also a considerable influence from other religions, such as Islam through the ages. Pankhurst further notes that the contact and influence of the neighbouring Arab culture and civilization has had considerable influence, and the activities of the missionaries of the various nationalities were also significant.

The history of educational language policies of Ethiopia can be broadly categorized into two historical periods: (1) traditional formal education, and (2) the era of modern education. The period of traditional formal education ranges approximately from the Axum period (1st century B.C.) to the end of the 19th century. During this long period, Ethiopia developed a system of traditional Church and Quranic schools. The second period, the era of modern education, begins in the early years of the 20th century. In what follows, we shall first briefly examine how each educational language policy, covert or overt, was tied to the political goals and philosophy of the period. Then, we shall review each policy and its achievements and drawbacks in the historical context in which it was implemented.

3.2. Traditional Formal Education

A detailed description of the history of education in Ethiopia has been given by Pankhurst (1976), while the Orthodox Church school system and the nature of Quranic schools have been described in detail by Haile Gebriel (1976). Teshome (1979) gives a comprehensive description of the foundation of modern education in Ethiopia in which he looks into the traditional church education in some detail and describes extensively the foundation and expansion of modern education until the 1974 revolution. The genesis and expansion of modern education and its impact on the social and political transformation in the 20th century is examined by Bahru (2002).

On the beginnings of traditional education, Teshome (1979, 10) comments, "Christianity, Islam, Judaism and Paganism have coexisted in Ethiopia for centuries, and all have founded schools for their adherents' children". All of them had their own geographical area of influence which contributed to the development of traditional education.

For centuries, the Ethiopian Orthodox Church, which was established in the fourth century A.D., provided the only schools, particularly in the highlands of Christian Ethiopia. It primarily provided a religious education that consisted, in its earlier stages, of learning to read and write and to recite a few biblical texts in Ge'ez (Pankhurst 1976, 305). Although church education was primarily aimed at producing priests, monks, and *debteras* (church scholars), it also trained state servants, such as judges, governors, scribes, treasurers, and administrators—thus meeting the human power and intellectual needs of church and state alike (Teshome 1979).

Another source of indigenous educational system, as Bahru (2002, 22) notes, was provided by Islam. Quranic schools in the Muslim-inhabited areas of the east and west of the country and also in Wollo since the 18th century enjoyed close ties with neighbouring Arab countries for many hundreds of years due to Ethiopia's relations with Islam dating back to the time of the Prophet Mohammed (Pankhurst 1976, 309). An early nineteenth-century traveller, Charles Johnston (Pankhurst 1976, 309–10), reported that there were a great number of Somalis and Dankalis, who had never resided in towns, but were able to read and write Arabic. Also an Egyptian officer, Muhammed Moktar (Pankhurst 1976, 310), reported that there were good Quranic schools in the walled city of Harar in 1875. He witnessed that education in the city of Harar was very well developed (*ibid*).

In the 19th century, the involvement of missionaries was still very limited. Pankhurst (1976, 310) notes, "The strength of Orthodox Ethiopian Christianity, and to a lesser extent Islam, greatly limited the impact of European missionaries who were in consequence far less successful in Ethiopia than in many other parts of Africa". An early attempt made in the sixteenth century to convert the country to the Roman Catholic faith had failed terribly and resulted in the expulsion of the Portuguese missionaries.

In 1830s, some missionaries ran a school in Shoa, and during the reign of Tewodros a small school was set up at Awra and later at Megdela. None of these efforts left any lasting effect on the country's educational system (Teshome 1979, 22).

For several centuries the Orthodox Church and the Quranic schools were the only institutions that provided formal education in Ethiopia. In its educational efforts, the church continued to use the Ge'ez language until the early decades of the twentieth century. Amharic has been in use perhaps since the 14th century along with Ge'ez but the formal teaching of Amharic as a subject began only in the early decades of the 20th century. Arabic has remained the language of literacy and religious studies in Quranic schools.

Amharic is believed to have replaced Ge'ez as the language of the imperial court during the 13th century, i.e. during the reign of Lalibela, who is believed to have lived from approximately 1160 to 1211 (Sergew 1969, 265). Other sources indicate that Ge'ez ceased to be a spoken language between the 9th and 12th centuries and hence various other languages rose to prominence (Cooper 1976, 289). The reason why Amharic gradually replaced Ge'ez, according to tradition, was that King Lalibela wanted to reward the Amharas who had assisted him in his ascent to power and who also made up the bulk of his military power. Historical sources indicate that the replacement of Ge'ez by Amharic is to be attributed to political and religious factors. Getatchew (2005) recounts, "Amharic gained prominence when the Axum dynasty was overthrown and the royal family took refuge among the Amharic-speaking population". According to him, following the transition of power from the Axum to the Zagwe dynasty, the ruling class become Amharic speakers, and this must have attracted Amharic speakers to the palace as functionaries and induced non-Amharas to adopt Amharic over the course of time. Furthermore, Getatchew argues, in the context of the religious rivalry between the Orthodox, Catholic and protestant religions, religious leaders were impelled to use Amharic in place of Ge'ez in order to win the hearts of their target population, the Amharic speakers.

Between the 13th and 17th centuries, the flowering period of Ge'ez literature, Ge'ez probably existed alongside Amharic in a diglossic relationship; "Ge'ez was reserved for literary, ecclesiastical, and ceremonial functions, and Amharic was used in the ordinary interactions of day-to-day life" (Cooper 1976, 289). Cooper further notes:

> The observation by the seventeenth century European scholar Ludolph that his very learned Ethiopian informant Gregory could not speak Giiz without mixing it with Amharic words indicates that in the Ethiopia of that day (and probably for hundreds of years before that), Giiz was not used for ordinary spoken purposes. On the other hand, Gregory found it even more difficult to write Amharic (Ullendorff 1965, 17) since that language was typically not used for written purposes.

The literary domination of Ge'ez was, however, challenged by the developments in the mid-19th century. Although popular songs in honour of the kings had been composed in Amharic as far back as the reigns of Yekuno Amlak (1270–1285), Amade Tsion (1314–1344), and Yeshaq (1413–1430), the mid-19th century witnessed the development of a new literary language, Amharic, that replaced Ge'ez in a shift away from the long-established tradition of using Ge'ez for literary purposes. This happened as a result of the policy of Emperor Tewodros; indeed Cooper (1976, 290) argues that the promotion of Amharic literature was part of his campaign to reunify Ethiopia. "Amharic became the accepted language of the imperial court and replaced Ge'ez as a language in which the Royal chronicles were written" (*ibid*). As Bahru (1991, 34) rightly puts it, "Culturally Tewodros's reign is significant because it witnessed the birth of a fairly well-developed literary Amharic". Tewodros was the first Ethiopian monarch to have the royal chronicles written in Amharic. His successor, the Emperor Yohannes IV (1871–1889), continued the use of Amharic, not his native tongue Tigrinya, at the royal court and for administration purposes as an instrument of national unification.

During the second half of the 19th century, Yohannes's successor Menelik, who was from the southernmost part of the Amharic-speaking area, expanded the Ethiopian territory to the south, southwest and the east. He incorporated into the Ethiopian Empire peoples and polities that had not been traditionally or continuously ruled by Ethiopian monarchs, such as the Oromo, the Harari, and the Somali. The use of Amharic spread with the expansion of the empire. Menelik's policy concerning the use of Amharic was to incorporate the elites without bothering to introduce Amharic to the ordinary people. Those assuming official positions in the government were expected to speak Amharic. The agents for the spread of Amharic were the high officials, members of the army, the clergy, and the *Balabats* (native chiefs who were and local representatives of the government).

The whole process did not emerge as a result of any carefully planned government policy, nor was Amharic ever defined as the official language of the Empire in the nineteenth century (Cohen 2000, 80). The language policy was a covert and de facto one with no explicit directives and regulations.

Although this period lacks a coherent and explicit policy towards the use of languages in formal education in particular, this does not mean that the policy was neutral with regard to the use of other languages in formal education. Amharic and to some extent Ge'ez were the primary languages used in formal education, business, state administration and the like. Ge'ez was the primary language used in the Christian areas while Arabic was used in Quranic schools as the language of literacy and religious studies in the famous Muslim schools in Wollo and Gondar.

The fact that Amharic, Ge'ez or Arabic was not legally protected, sanctioned, promoted, etc. does not mean that other languages were free to take over their position and function as languages of formal education or state administration. The real truth lies not in what may be legally and officially stated but in the subtler workings of what Schiffman (1996) calls the 'covert and implicit policy'. From this practice, one can see that the policy was not linguistically tolerant and did not accept multilingualism. The seeds of monolingualism were thus clearly inherent in the Ethiopian linguistic culture. The default language of state administration was Amharic, with some provision for the other two religious languages, Ge'ez and Arabic.

Hence, the covert language policy was not neutral since it clearly favoured the Amharic language and used Amharic as a tool for unification of the nation. This was evident in the promotion of Amharic as a literary language, in place of Ge'ez, by Emperor Tewodros. Schiffman (1996, 213) asserts that no statute or constitutional amendment or regulatory law is necessary to maintain this kind of covert policy. The strength of the policy lies in the society's basic assumptions and beliefs or ideology about the given language.

3.3. The Era of Modern Education

Modern education was introduced into Ethiopia at the beginning of the 20th century as a part of the modernization and nation building effort. Since then, Ethiopian education has passed through five roughly distinct periods:

1) The early 20th century can be characterized as the 'permissive' period in the history of Ethiopian education due to the significant level of tolerance in the use of various local and international languages in formal education.

2) The period of Italian occupation (1936–1941) can be seen as a colonial policy of segregation where schools were divided between natives and Italians, limiting the participation of natives. The use of

local languages in the school system was allowed "not as a pedagogically sound first step but as a means of repression" (McNabb 1984, 5). The Italians formulated, proclaimed and implemented an elaborate language policy. The "national" or official language of their empire, Italian East Africa (which included Ethiopia, Eritrea and Somalia), was Italian. In each of the five regions of the empire (Eritrea, Amhara, the present day Oromia-Sidama, Harar, Somalia), Tigrinya, Amharic, Oromo, Arabic and Somali were respective official second languages. Other languages, such as Wolayitta and Kefinoonoo were also recognized in some of the sub regions. These local languages were used in administration and basic education alongside Italian (Pankhurst 1976, 322).

3) The Post-WWII period (1941–1974) witnessed a diametrically opposed policy to that of the earliest period, and can be labelled, following Baker (1996, 170), as the 'dismissive or repudiation' period: it followed an autocratic, centrist, unilingual policy regarding the use of local languages in formal education.

4) The period of the military government (1974–1991) was a kind of assimilationist transitional period in bilingual education, where other languages were officially recognized and a good many languages were used in non-formal education, such as mass literacy and mass media.

5) The current language policy (1991– to date) can be described as 'pluralist' or maintenance/heritage bilingual education, which claims to satisfy the demands of self-expression for Ethiopia's various ethnic groups and is intended to produce equity in terms of basic education.

We now turn to the discussion of the development of formal education during each individual period, its defining characteristics and the type of policies adopted regarding the use of languages in education, and the ideologies in which these policies were rooted.

3.3.1. The Early Decades of the 20th Century (1908–1935)

The Ethiopian government decided in the early 20th century to introduce modern education. Emperor Menelik was very keen on education and his attitude is clearly revealed by his discussion with the first American envoy on the possibility of training Ethiopians in the US. He was quoted as saying: "our young men must be educated" (quoted in Pankhurst 1976, 315). Menelik's view was summed up by Achaber (1931, 32), quoted in Pankhurst (1976, 315), who stated, "Ethiopia needed educated people to ensure our peace, to reconstruct our country and to enable it to exist as a great nation in the face of European powers". Menelik's ideology concerning language and education was deeply rooted in the mission of modernization of the state. The first significant step, i.e. the opening of the first modern school in the palace compound, was taken by the Emperor himself. The school taught reading, writing, calligraphy, religion, Ethiopian history, law, and Ge'ez (Rosen 1907, 267 quoted in Pankhurst 1976, 315).

Menelik's attempts to establish modern schools were met with some resistance by the Orthodox Church; nevertheless, he managed to recruit some ten Egyptians in 1906, and opened Ethiopia's first government-operated modern school, the Ecole Imperiale Menelik II, in October 1908 in Addis Ababa, and another school in the same year in Harar. Other schools followed and were established in regional capitals. Menelik's determination to introduce modern education was vividly stated in the famous proclamation he issued in 1905. It reads,

> "In other countries, not only do they learn, even more they make new things. Therefore, from now on after reaching the age of six, boys and girls must be sent to school. As for parents who would not send their children to school, when the former die, their wealth, instead of reverting to their children, will be transferred to the Government. My government will prepare the schools and the teachers".

The first decade of the 20th century was, therefore, significant in the development of modern education in Ethiopia. That period also witnessed the development of non-government schools; about 100 private schools sprang up in Addis Ababa alone (Pankhurst 1976, 315; see Bahru (2002) for a detailed description of the expansion of schools, and Tekeste (1990) for a brief historical outline).

Following the opening of schools, a number of other factors accelerated the development of modern education during the first decade of the century. The establishment of the first printing press (Pankhurst 1968, 676–7), the production of teaching materials by foreign-educated Ethiopians, e.g. Michael Birru's first mathematics books in Amharic (Cohen 1915; ccvi and passim), and the founding of the first Amharic newspaper A'miro (Pankhurst 1962, vi, 262) were among the major agents for the spread of modern education in Ethiopia.

The medium of instruction in government schools was mainly French. It seems that this was not the result of a premeditated and planned language policy but emerged from circumstances. When Menelik decided to import teachers from abroad with the aim of establishing modern education, he was faced by opposition from the Orthodox Church (Mahtema Sellasie 1942, 616 quoted in Pankhurst 1976, 316), especially by the bishop Abune Matteos, who was an Egyptian. In order to overcome objections from the church, Menelik adopted the policy of recruiting teachers from among the Copts of Egypt, apparently as a compromise solution, and in accordance with the practice in Egypt, the language of instruction in Ethiopia became French.

Girma (1963, 335–336) rightly describes this period of Ethiopian education as an 'imitation stage', where western educational systems were directly imported without any effort at adaptation to local needs and conditions; this was manifested in the kind of buildings that were erected, the kind of curriculum that was adopted, and the foreign teachers. Girma further notes, "in spite of the unsoundness of the procedure, much gain resulted from this first attempt to introduce outside education into Ethiopia. Within a few years, Ethiopia was able to produce many educated young men who were prepared to take up important government posts". This was clearly in line with the ideology and political aim of the government.

Another important development of this period was the involvement of missionaries in the establishment of modern education. Missionary activities increased particularly after the First World War, despite the stiff resistance from the Orthodox Church, and in 1935 there were about 100 mission stations in different parts of the country who were engaged in a certain amount of teaching (Haile Gabriel 1976, 366; McNabb 1984, 4). Among these were the Lazarists, who by then operated four schools in Addis Ababa and Alitena, with instruction in French and Amharic; the Capuchins, who ran seven secondary schools, twenty-four primary schools and fourteen orphanages, and who taught in English, French and Amharic; Other Roman Catholics, who ran considerable number of schools in Addis, Harar, Dire Dawa and Sofi, in French and Amharic. On the Lutheran side, the Swedish Evangelical Mission ran eight schools and the Swedish Friends of the Bible Mission had three schools in Addis, with instruction in Amharic, Oromo, English and French. The Seventh Day Adventists had a school in Addis, and a smaller institution at Addis Alem and they gave instruction entirely in Amharic in both schools. The United Presbyterian Church of North America established a school at Sayo (western Ethiopia) and gave instruction in Oromo (Pankhurst 1976, 317).

In 1927, when Tafari Makonnen, later Emperor Haile Sellasie, opened the Tafari Makennen School, the education given was markedly French-oriented. This was because most of the teaching staff members were French people and French-speaking Lebanese (Pankhurst 1976, 315).

Although French was the dominant language of instruction, other international languages, such as English and Italian, and local languages, such as Amharic, Oromo and Tigrinya, were also used in the school system. There seems to have been no explicit overt language policy at the time; in a way, it was a kind of multilingual approach to basic education. The underlying ideology behind the de facto policy was the very strong zeal for modernizing and building a strong nation in the face of the European powers. This nationalist attitude and covert language and educational policy was clearly revealed when Tafari Makonnen delivered his opening speech in 1927 at the inauguration of the spacious and modern school built by himself and named after him. Pankhurst (1976, 318) quoted Ras Tafari saying,

> ...the time had passed for mere lip-service to the country, and that the crying need of the people was for education, without which they could not

maintain their independence. The proof of real patriotism, he declared, was therefore the founding of schools. Progress, he averred, could be carried out only little by little; for his own part he had built the school as a beginning and as an example, and appealed to the wealthy among the people to follow.

With the expansion of schools French became the preferred language of instruction, and Amharic enjoyed a special status. The Amharic language was the language of government and administration and Amharic writing and reading skills were the main entry requirement to all government schools. Ge'ez was also accorded a special status, as the official language of the Orthodox Church, and continued to serve as the language of literacy and religious studies. Arabic had the same status as Ge'ez in Muslim communities throughout the country.

Clearly, this period can be labelled up to a point as the 'permissive period' in the use of local languages in formal education. As demonstrated by the media of instruction adopted in the various schools (French, English, Amharic, Italian, Oromo), linguistic diversity was tolerated and the use of different languages as media of instruction was accepted. In some of these schools the approach of 'dual language education' or even 'multiple language education' was permitted. So long as it helped to promote the ideology and political aim of the government, i.e. the mission of modernization and building a strong nation, the language of instruction or the use of local languages in formal education did not become an issue. In other words, multilingualism or linguistic diversity per se was not considered a problem for the nation-building mission envisaged by the government.

3.3.2. The Italian Occupation (1936–1941)

In 1936, when Fascist Italy invaded Ethiopia, there were some 21 government schools and the infrastructure for modern education was already securely laid (Teshome 1979, 42). The positive development towards multilingual education was interrupted by the Italian occupation, which resulted in total disruption of the pattern of language use in education and a closing of missionary activities. It was a dramatic reversal of policy, entrenched in colonial ideology. Between the years of 1936 and 1941, a policy was enacted in which natives were to be provided with only elementary education, and to this effect an edict of 1936 divided the Italian East African Empire into six administrative units, with languages of education: Tigrinya in Eritrea; Amharic in Amhara; Amharic and Oromo in Addis Ababa; Harari and Arabic in Harar; Oromo and Kefinoonoo in Oromia; Somali in Somalia (Italy, Ministero delle Colonie 1937). This policy was put into practice for some five years from 1936/37 to 1940/41. Although this was only a short time period, it marked a significant departure from the past.

3.3.3. Post-WWII Period (1941–1974)

In the 1940s, English replaced French as the most common medium of instruction for education in Ethiopia, as a result of its increasing global significance and in recognition of its widespread international use. With the expanded post-war use of English, British influence was widespread not only due to the British help in the liberation from the Italian invasion but also due to Britain's colonial ambition to exert political dominance over the country. Girma (1963, 338) reports that after the liberation, the important advisors of the Ministry of Education were British; the headmasterships of schools in Addis Ababa were monopolized by the British; and the textbooks were brought mainly from Britain and its East African colonies. Girma proposes that the first nine years after the liberation of the country be characterized as "the pioneering stage" as the Ministry of Education was in a state of uncertainty regarding educational language policy; it was a time of experimentation. This period was followed by various attempts to adapt education to the conditions, needs, problems and aspirations of the country; and these attempts were fostered by undertaking pioneering basic research under the American influence of what was known as the 'Point Four Scheme'. According to Girma (1963, 339), this programme can be credited with encouraging research in Ethiopia, with a view to adapting education to local conditions with the help of funds and experts provided by the American government. The influence thereby shifted from the British to the Americans. One such notable influence was the extension of the six-year elementary school to eight years, following the American model.

By 1950s, there were enough qualified Ethiopians, both in schools and in the bureaucracy, to assume the positions of foreign teachers and advisors, which eventually, according to Girma (1963, 339), brought to the fore the vital issue of the language of instruction, i.e. the idea of replacing English by Amharic. As already pointed out, after the liberation, English was recognized as the official foreign language of the country and it was also stipulated by the Ministry of Education that English be the medium of instruction for all subjects. This policy continued unchallenged until the 1950s, i.e. until Amharic emerged as a rival and heralded the beginning of the policy of 'Ethiopianization'. The struggle between Amharic and English continued for some time. Finally, in 1963, the Ministry of Education decided that Amharic should replace English as medium of instruction for primary education in all government schools as a reflection of policies intended to encourage national integration and development sponsored by the government of Haile Sellassie *(ibid)*. It is worth noting that this change of the status quo was the result of continued nationalist pressure for using an indigenous language, in this case Amharic, for reasons of sentimental attachment, authenticity and efficiency.

The position of Amharic as the official language was enshrined in the 1930 Constitution as well as in the 1955 Revised Constitution (IGE 1955), Article

125, and was strengthened by legislation. All the official functions of the government were conducted in Amharic. All printed materials were produced in Amharic and to some degree in Tigrinya. The use of Amharic was also well-established in the judicial system. It was during this period that Ethiopia had its first explicit official (legislated) language policy.

In order to institutionalize the dominance of the Amharic language, the National Amharic Language Academy was established in 1972 with the sole objective of fostering the growth of the Amharic language and encouraging the development of Amharic literature (Negarit Gazeta 1972). While the other Ethiopian languages were ignored, Ge'ez was given special attention to preserve its ecclesiastical literature. This neglect of the other major languages of the nation is believed to have been one of the causes of dissatisfaction during the monarchy.

The Ethiopian educational language policy of this period appears to have been influenced by two factors. Firstly, the pre-WWII education system of Ethiopia had been markedly French-oriented; this now changed fundamentally. Secondly, Haile Sellassie intensified his policy of centralization after WWII; and his language and educational policy may well have been part and parcel of this policy of centralization, as language policies are very often part of a larger social and political policy. In the French language policy of France, for instance, the law requires the exclusive use of the national language (i.e. French) in all public and private acts, from the drafting of laws to the language of commercial transactions and even a private citizen's last will (Schiffman 1996). In the same way, in Article 14 of Negarit Gazeta 1944, the first explicit official (legislated) language policy states that the official language of the Empire is Amharic.

After the war, missionary activities continued with the support of the Emperor himself, who saw them as partners in his modernization and nation-building mission. But the activity of the missionaries was not left unchecked, and the government issued new directives to control the missionaries. Article 13 of the government directive controlling foreign missions decreed, "The general language of instruction throughout Ethiopia shall be the Amharic language, which all missionaries will be expected to learn".

The government also made a concession regarding language use in mission schools:

> In open areas missionaries may use orally local languages in the early stages of missionary work until such time as pupils and missionaries in Open Areas shall have a working knowledge of the Amharic language. The local languages may be used in the course of ordinary contacts with the local population (Negarit Gazeta 1944, Article 14).

The directives were not meant to discourage missionary activity as such. The aim was to bring this activity firmly in line with the aims of the government. Missionaries were charged with promoting the ideology of the government, and were expelled if they fail to do so. The restriction of missionaries to "open areas", areas not traditionally under the domination of the Ethiopian Orthodox Church, was part of a strategy for providing education without exhausting meagre state resources. The missionaries were given the more difficult task of educating entirely illiterate populations, who were not Amharic speakers.

Haile Sellasie's policy from WWII until he was overthrown by the military in 1974 was thus a repressive, centrist, monolingual policy decreed from above. It was handed down and strictly controlled by a highly centralized state. The policy had its roots in nation-building, unification and modernization, which was the underlying ideology of the period.

The policy may be characterized as 'dismissive' in nature; it reflected an 'Amharic only' attitude whose goal was to establish Amharic monolingualism and cultural assimilation—Amharic being used as a tool in advancing the ideology of the government. The strategy and the concomitant goal are thus to be considered as assimilation and centralization rather than 'Amharanization' per se (cf. Cohen 2000). Language was used here as scapegoat to advance the ideology of the political system of the day. Haile Sellassie dismissed the use of multiple languages in early formal education in favour of Amharic. The relentlessly monolingual policy pursued by the government recognized no equal for the Amharic language and brooked no opposition. Given the continued centralization of power in the capital, with little regional autonomy or authority including school policy, it is no wonder that regional languages in Ethiopia felt trodden under the weight of the national language. No right to early education through a minority language was acknowledged during that period.

A few months before the military takeover in 1974, the government of Haile Selassie considered changes affecting the status of the languages in the country. Amharic was retained as the official language of the state as spelled out in Article 4 of the Draft Constitution of 1974 (MGRE 1974), which reads, "The Amharic language remains as the official language of the nation". On the other hand, the other Ethiopian languages were officially recognized for the first time in the history of the country. Article 45 of the draft constitution reads, "Ethnic groups and nationalities have the right to preserve, develop, and modernize their languages and cultures".

This constitution never materialized; it was overtaken by time. It should be underlined, however, that the constitutional reform, proposed during the eleventh hour by the monarchy, was in effect an acknowledgement of the reality on the ground.

3.3.4. The Military Government (1974–1991)

The Derg military regime that replaced the monarchy declared itself from the outset to be a revolutionary socialist government. The policy adopted towards education was based on the ideology of Marxism-Leninism and guided by socialist principles and values. The education system was expected to precipitate a 'cultural revolution', which would alter the mind-set of the people in order to eradicate negative traditional practices, such as superstition, fetishism, obscurantism and witchcraft, and 'anti-revolutionary' attitudes, such as tribalism, regionalism, individualism and elitism. In the end, the education system would develop a new socialist citizen.

The military regime adopted an educational policy that systematically suppressed or marginalized traditional institutions (e.g. religious institutions) and challenged almost all forms of traditional culture, which were regarded as negative and anti-revolutionary. This was based on the assumption that, in traditional societies, given their characteristically low level of consciousness, religion, superstition and similar practices, take the place of science and block scientific analysis of the material and social milieu in favour of the supernatural. Claiming that education under the monarchy had created passivity, the Derg in response embraced the socialist ideology and imported an 'alien' policy to deal with the age-old problems of a feudal society. The ideological perception was that the education system under the monarchy had served 'feudalists' and 'imperialists' for furthering their interests and encouraging the belief in the infallibility of the older generations personified in elderly people, whose ideas remained unchallenged. Within the range of traditional values to be eliminated in the new system were, for example, male domination of women and related sexist values, and submission of young people to the chiefs or elderly people. In order to raise 'the low level of consciousness' of the masses and to disseminate the values of Marxism and Leninism and to radicalize the peasantry in particular, at the end of 1974 the Derg launched a programme called "Development through Cooperation, Enlightenment and Work Campaign", in which about 60,000 students and their teachers in institutions of higher learning and in the last two grades of secondary school participated. This campaign also served as a prelude to a much more vigorous literacy campaign launched in 1979.

Education under the military regime was meant to promote a new culture with a new ideology dictated by the ideals of socialism. By adopting this strategy, the Derg hoped to create what has been referred to as 'a new socialist citizen', that is, a society engineered to further the interests of the proletariat-peasant alliance, with a unified national identity and a scientific, materialist and dialectical outlook.

Soon after the Derg came to power, it nationalized all schools in order to create a favourable political context for meaningful educational transformation, and in 1975 non-governmental private schools, which accounted for over 14 per cent of the total enrolments in primary and secondary schools at the time of the Revolution, were transferred by proclamation to public ownership (Legesse 1984, 334). However, this measure imposed intolerable pressure on the educational sector associated with the increase of the school population. Although the process of nationalization was hailed as a major victory, the effective and immediate control of the education process required enormous efforts for which the government had insufficient human and material resources.

As part of this process, a radical change in the language policy was introduced, involving the recognition of the need to develop other languages, other than Amharic, in the area of literacy and to some extent in the mass media. At the time the Derg came to power, the illiteracy rate was estimated to be 93 per cent and the first success was seen when five major languages (Oromo, Wolaytta, Somali, Amharic and Tigrinya) were introduced in literacy programmes during the first phase in 1979. In the second phase, i.e. May 1981, five other languages (Hadiyya, Tigre, Kunama, Gedeo and Kambatta) were introduced. In the third phase, i.e. May 1982, Sidamo, Afar, Silt'i, Saho and Kefa-Mocha were also included. Hence, literacy was taught in 15 languages until the fall of the Derg regime.

It was thus in 1979, when the large-scale literacy campaign was launched, that the "National Amharic Language Academy" was replaced by "The Academy of Ethiopian Languages", another positive, pluralistic step towards recognizing other Ethiopian languages. As remarked, the period 1979–82 witnessed the use of 15 languages in literacy which was formerly limited to just the Amharic language. It is believed that these 15 languages satisfied the requirements of about 90 per cent of the Ethiopian population.

In order to meet the objectives of the new language policy, the Academy was reorganized into four units: (1) Lexicography, (2) Linguistics, (3) Terminology, and (4) Literature. The units were aimed at developing, modernizing, codifying and upgrading the various languages of Ethiopia. Until 1974 the only written languages were only Amharic and Tigrinya. The activities of the Academy of Ethiopian Languages and its reorganization with a new policy were genuine efforts towards institutionalizing the study of the multiplicity of languages of Ethiopia for modern purposes, such as basic education and mass media.

The ideological foundation upon which this policy rested was spelled out in sections 4a and 5 of the programme of the Marxist government. It reads:

> The rights of self-determination of all nationalities will be recognized and fully respected. No nationality will dominate another one since the history, culture, language and religion of each nationality will have equal recognition in accordance with the spirit of socialism.
>
> Within its environs, it (each nationality) has the right to determine the contents of its political, economic and social life, use its own language and elect its own leaders and administrators to its internal organs.

Clearly influenced by the Marxist ideology of the Soviet Union, the policy reflected a drive for the population to take up the ideology of socialism.

Critics say that the use of local languages was confined to non-formal education; in the area of mass literacy campaign and in the mass media. Amharic remained the only official language and the medium of instruction beyond basic literacy classes. Education was not only linked to the ideology of the power structure but also bound up with the challenge of building national unity, and the Derg, like its predecessor, hoped to create a unified sense of nationhood through the school system by using Amharic as a national language and as the only medium of instruction. Thus, the policy continued to be based on the ideology of assimilation, which was considered as a solid basis for nation-building.

Elements underlying the policy were, therefore, 'centralization' through the use of Amharic and 'duality of state language policy' observed in formal vs. informal education. The policy reflected the established attitude towards Amharic: the continued strengthening of the position of Amharic suited the purposes of the government, i.e. centralization. As the government actively sought to establish more effective forms of central control, Amharic proved to be a powerful tool in this process. This approach, it seems clear, underestimated the complexity of the Ethiopian socio-cultural reality.

3.3.5. The Present Language Policy (1991–to date)

Following the change of government in 1991, several vernaculars were introduced in formal primary education and other official purposes as part of a wider reorganization of geopolitical and administrative structures in Ethiopia that has placed language at the centre of the process of social redefinition. According to the current constitutional framework in force in Ethiopia, all of Ethiopia's constituent languages, of which there are at least 80, may be used for a range of official purposes. The Constitution of the Federal Democratic Republic of Ethiopia (FDRE 1995), Article 5, states:

- All Ethiopian languages shall enjoy equal state recognition;
- Amharic shall be the working language of the Federal Government; and
- Members of the Federation may by law determine their respective working languages.

More specifically, the constitution spells out in Article 39 the rights of Nations Nationalities and Peoples as follows:

- Every Nation, Nationality and People in Ethiopia has an unconditional right to self-determination, including the right to secession;
- Every Nation, Nationality and People in Ethiopia has the right to speak, to write and develop its own language; to express, to develop and to promote its culture; and to preserve its history;

- Every Nation, Nationality and People has the right to a full measure of self-government which includes the right to establish institutions of government in the territory that it inhabits and to equitable representation in state and Federal governments; and
- A 'Nation, Nationality or People' for the purposes of this constitution, is a group of people who have or share a large measure of a common culture or similar customs, mutual intelligibility of language, belief in a common or related identities, a common psychological make-up, and who inhabit an identifiable, predominantly contiguous territory.

The educational and training policy of Ethiopia, issued in 1994 by the Ministry of Education, states the overall strategy concerning vernacular education as follows:

- Cognizant of the pedagogical advantage of the child in learning in mother tongue and the rights of nationalities to promote the use of their languages, primary education will be given in Nationality languages;
- Making the necessary preparation, nations and nationalities can learn in their own language or can choose from among those selected on the basis of national and countrywide distribution;
- The language of teacher training for kindergarten and primary education will be the nationality language used in the area;
- Amharic shall be taught as a language of countrywide communication;
- English will be the medium of instruction for secondary and higher education;
- Pupils can choose and learn at least one nationality language and one foreign language for cultural and international relations; and
- English will be taught as a subject starting from grade one.

Individual concrete initiatives to introduce and integrate the vernaculars into the school system, however, are effectively decided at the regional level, and at times at the zonal and district levels. In most regions in Ethiopia, in addition to the vernacular, which is used as the medium of instruction at the primary level, Amharic, the official language of the country, and English are taught as subjects within the primary school system. English is introduced as of grade one in parallel with the vernacular, whereas Amharic is given as a subject starting from grade three. The introduction of English, which is a foreign language, before the introduction of the country's official language projects an ideological stance towards the status of the two languages.

The implementing entities are the various branches of the government structures and the society. The language group formulates the request, provides the language speakers for production of the teaching materials, and the teachers. Political entities at all level evaluate the request and give permission to implement; they initiate the political process for a choice of the script (Roman or Ethiopic). Education bureaus at the regional, zonal, and district levels prepare the curriculum materials based on the national syllabus, and monitor teacher training. Teacher-training institutions provide training to teach the different languages both as subjects and as media of instruction.

Since the more than 80 languages of Ethiopia cannot all be introduced from one day to the next, especially as many of the languages are not yet written, some kind of criteria must be set in order to make use of the available resources in an effective way. The conditions for implementation include: demographically and politically important languages get first consideration; the nationality has to show that they have the necessary human power and financial capability in the region; and initiative and pressure from the population of a given nationality language group may influence the speed of implementation.

Both the Derg and the current government were strongly influenced by the notion of "nationality rights" and the idea of "self-determination". Although they share the same ideological philosophy, as rightly outlined by Hoben (1995, 188), the present government differs from the Derg in the following ways.

1) In promoting "nationality languages", it has switched from a non-formal programme to the formal education system;

2) Cushitic languages, such as Oromo and a dozen others are written in Latin script; and

3) It has undertaken a complete reorganization of administrative units based on language and ethnicity.

It has now been more than a decade since the policy was first implemented. Although so far no concrete study has fully evaluated the implementation model adopted by each region, there are some research results that both confirm the positive achievements of the policy and also express concerns about the use of different languages in the primary education system.

In light of UNESCO's (1953) declaration and concerns for 'linguistic human rights, the government's policy has been considered as a step in the right direction (see Skutnabb-Kangas and Phillipson 1995; Bloor and Wondwosen 1996). Major problems, however, have also been identified in the area of human power, curriculum development, teaching materials, language standardization and orthographic development (Boother and Walker 1997). More specifically, the policy has been regarded as potentially politically divisive since it allegedly shows the government's intention to divide the country along ethnic lines, thereby contributing to its hidden agenda of "erosion of the existing bases of national unity" (Cohen

2000). It has also been argued that the policy limits freedom of mobility across administrative units or federal structures, thereby disturbing the existing patterns of contact between different peoples and nationalities and limiting economic opportunities. Despite the claims of the policy, it has been argued that it is inherently unequal and unfair because some will have less access to participation in the political, social and economic life of the nation as compared to those who are educated in Amharic. Furthermore, it has been stated that the policy perpetuates ethnic enclaves and encourages narrow formulations of identity. No public consultations have been made to establish popular support for the policy, and the great speed with which the reform was introduced has been questioned. The policy suffers from ambiguity on the division of roles and responsibilities between federal and regional offices dealing with education (Tekeste 1990). Overemphasis on English at the expense of the official national language (which is used all over the country as a lingua franca) has also been seen as a major weakness of the policy.

3.4. Achievements and Challenges: Perspectives

In the preceding sections, attempt are made to give an overview of the history of educational language policies in Ethiopia and the ideological stances reflected in the successive political systems in relation to the use of languages in education. Accordingly, we looked into the types of educational language policies adopted over the history of the country, the basic characteristics of these policies, the major changes that occurred and the causes of these changes. In the foregoing discussion, the history of educational language policy in Ethiopia was divided roughly into six different periods that were marked successively (and respectively) by the following characteristics: (1) pre-modern religious-based traditional education, (2) the fairly tolerant pluralist policy of early modern education, (3) the Italian colonial policy of segregation, (4) an autocratic monolingual education, (5) the revolutionary socialist type, and (6) the present multilingual pluralist policy.

The ideological basis of these perspectives and outlooks revolves around the myths developed about the concept of multilingualism in general and multilingual education in particular. One such widespread myth alleges that 'multilingualism is a barrier to nation building process and development', an outlook which has its roots in the false association of language with ethnicity (Bamgbose 1991, 14). This distrust of multilingualism, and the corollary effect of reluctance to accept and recognize linguistic diversity, has led to the belief that the best model for national integration and nation building is the use of a single common language. The one-language policy and the consequent process of enforced linguistic assimilation were therefore advocated as a strategy for nation-building and modernization process.

In traditional Ethiopia, the one-language policy, i.e. the practice of using a single language, Ge'ez, as the language of the empire, the *Lisane Nigus* (literally 'the language of the King'), evolved into a diglossic situation with the recognition of Amharic as the official language of the country whilst Ge'ez assumed the status of the literary language until the second half of the 19th century. The change of the status quo is interesting for at least two reasons. First, it was the language of the ordinary people that replaced the more prestigious literary language as the official language of the nation. Second, the transition was from a unilingual policy to a bilingual one that recognized the language of the masses, a policy that was able to bridge the gap between the elite and the masses. The policy was evidently an attempt to achieve a kind of compromise between having a highly developed indigenous literary language for the elite and a widespread unwritten language spoken by the masses; the goal was to attain efficiency in the smooth running of government activities. The continued use of a literary language as the language of the state, in a society where illiteracy was very high, would have left the gap between the elite and the masses as wide as ever. The promotion of Amharic to a full-fledged literary language by Emperor Tewodros in the second half of the 19th century surely resulted from his awareness of the gap between the elite and the ordinary citizenry.

During the era of modern education, especially in the first decades of the 20th century, there was a significant degree of tolerance towards multilingualism, linguistic diversity, and multilingual education, as demonstrated in the use of multiple languages even in the same school. The ideology of the time was a form of nationalism dominated by the quest for building a strong nation in the face of European colonial powers. It is interesting, then, that the strategy adopted was not at all a one-language policy of assimilation, as might have been expected, but more of a pluralist approach. The widespread myth that multilingualism impedes national integration was not a view held by the political system of the time; linguistic diversity was not perceived to be a divisive element which would exacerbate ethnic tensions or hinder national integration. Hence, in the school system multiple languages, both local and international, were used for providing basic education. However, this positive development towards multilingual education was disrupted by the Italian occupation of 1936.

Between the period of WWII and the 1974 revolution, a period in which modern education flourished throughout the country, various important policy decisions were made and put into action. The language of instruction was moved first from French to English and then, with the introduction of the political philosophy of "Ethiopianization', English was replaced by Amharic in all elementary schools. The political ideology was a nationalist ideology that strove toward the goal of having an indigenous language as national language, for reasons of sentimental attachment and authenticity. It was a gradualist approach; however, since Amharic was limited to elementary education and English continued to serve as the language of higher education. Amharic, a language claimed to have been spoken by a third of the population at the time, was also considered to adequately fulfil the role of language of wider communication, which was a necessity in order to run the country in an efficient manner. The paradox within this ideology was that the political philosophy of 'Ethiopianization' was advanced only through Amharic, thereby excluding around two-thirds of the masses who could not fully participate because the language of the government, and hence the language of basic education, was not available to them. The grass-roots participation of the masses in social and political affairs that should be envisaged by any nation-building and modernizing ideology were not achieved due to the very low level of literacy, in spite of the persistent efforts made by the government of Haile Sellassie to promote and expand modern education in Ethiopia.

The following statement by Bamgbose (1991, 75) clearly delineates the scenario that the Ethiopian education system, like many of the developing countries', had to face.

> ...the existing school systems in the Third World countries have served only to train tiny elites to run a bureaucracy and the modern sector of an economy while neglecting the training of human resources capable of stimulating production in areas essential to the majority of the population. For this situation, grass-roots education will be needed, and the use of several indigenous languages would seem to be inevitable.

The achievement of the post-WWII period can only be seen in the 'horizontal integration' it has made, i.e. an integration involving a combination of the segment of the educated elite from each of the different ethnic or linguistic groups in the country. As Bamgbose (1991, 18) rightly points out, "the question is whether national integration should be equated with the integration of the elites".

The period of the military government was, in many ways, a continuation of the earlier approach of advancing a one-language policy and a strategy of assimilation, except that it was based on socialist political philosophy and values. The system, however, made an admirable attempt regarding the need to bridge the gulf between the elite and the masses by launching a large-scale mass literacy programme using 15 vernacular languages, which was claimed to satisfy the needs of 90 per cent of the population. It was a transitional measure taken by the power structure to change a linguistic landscape that was entirely dominated by Amharic and to mobilize the masses along socialist lines. However, the policy fell short of its promises of incorporating the vernacular into the formal education system. The policy continued to be governed by considerations of nationalism, i.e. maintaining an indigenous language as a national language and adopting it as the language of wider communication for the efficient running of the country.

The educational language policy of the current government, like that of the Derg, is committed to the principles of "self-determination" and the "rights of nationalities". However, the two regimes differ, among other things, in the extent and degree of self-determination that each regime actually granted to regions and geo-political units. The present government has advanced a multilingual policy far more rigorously than ever before. As a result, currently there are 22 vernaculars in use in the Ethiopian school system, one of which is the Harari language.

This takes us to the subject of the present study, the Harari geopolitical unit, one of the nine regional states within the current federal system of Ethiopia. The following section examines the politics and patterns of contact in Harari since its incorporation into the Ethiopian empire in 1887.

3.5. Politics and Patterns of Contact

The emergence of Harar is closely tied to the advent and expansion of Islam in eastern and south-eastern Ethiopia in the early 12th century A.D. It came into prominence as a leading Islamic political and commercial centre in the region during the wars of Ahmed Ibn Ibrahim, commonly known as Ahmed *Gragn*) (the left-handed) (Trimingham 1976, 62–63; 85). With the death of Ahmed Gragn in 1543, Harar's military might have gone to an end. To make matters worse, Oromo encroachment forced Harar to contract into a tiny city-state. In an attempt to stem the rising tide of Oromo pressure, Nur Ibn al-Wazir Mujahid, who became the Amir of Harar in 1551/52, erected a strong wall around the city (*ibid.* 91, 96). However, that did not bring peace and tranquillity to Harar. The ever-increasing threat from the Oromo and the internal feuds within the ruling family forced the rulers of Harar to transfer their seat of power to Awsa in the Afar lowlands in 1577. For the next seventy years, Harar was no longer the political centre of the state of Adal. The foundation of a new dynasty in 1647 by Ali ibn Dawid rescued Harar from its obscurity and restored its status as a city-state. Although its heyday as capital of a powerful state had gone forever, it witnessed a succession of many Amirs right up to its occupation by an Egyptian army in October 1875. Following the end of the ten-year Egyptian occupation, the local dynasty was restored and ruled Harar until the beginning of 1887. Finally in early January of 1887, Menilek's army defeated the forces of the last Amir, Abdullahi, at Chelenqo and incorporated Harar into the Ethiopian empire (Caulk 1977, 369; 1971, 16-17; Abir 1968, 9).

Since 1887, Harar has passed through different historical epochs under the successive regimes that have ruled Ethiopia. Immediately after its incorporation into the Ethiopian empire, Harari lost its political sovereignty but to some extent, at least initially, its people were allowed to participate in the administration of Harar. Carmichael (2001) recounts that after the incorporation of Harar, unlike in other subjugated areas, the Ethiopian government inherited and retained the long-established administrative structures and official archives. The archives were a concrete witness to the fact that Harari officials used literacy as a tool of governance in the pre-conquest eras. Astutely, the new government, instead of destroying or changing the administrative structures, opted for using them to rule Harari, and appointed both local and immigrant officials. The Harari officials were retained partly because the documents of important institutions of Harari, which were the backbone of the Harari administration, were written in Arabic, a language the new immigrants were not familiar with. As a result, important administrative institutions, such as the *Diwan*[1] and *Afersata*[2] and, as a consequence, local politicians who were able to operate within these institutions were retained under the new governor's office led by Ras Mekonnen, Emperor Haile Sellasie's father.

During the reign of Haile Sellassie, with the Ethiopian state more highly centralized than ever, Harar was put under the Hararge province which also included the Ogaden region. The Harari were subject to the assimilationist policy of the political system and were forced to integrate into the mainstream political, social, and economic structures.

The Derg regime that replaced the monarchy made little difference to the Harari's, who had continued to resent the increasing number of mostly Christian immigrants, the fast-growing land confiscations through various means, and the endangered ethnic identity of the Harari. During the revolution, the nationalization of land and other properties as well as the forcible conscription of Harari youth further weakened the Harari ethnic identity. This led to the perception that the change of the monarchy to the military regime was little more than a transition from the frying pan into the fire.

The current government with its political ideology of 'ethnic federalism' has given the Harari unprecedented concessions in the Federal parliament as well as in the Regional government. For instance, the Harari ethnic group represents the region in the Federal parliament though it constitutes only seven per cent of the total population of the region. According to Article 25/2, 1995 of the Constitution of the Harari Regional Government, members of the Harari National Congress shall be elected from candidates of Harari ethnicity only, whether they are living in Harari Region or settled elsewhere in different regions of Ethiopia. This same congress has been given the sole power to nominate candidates for the President of the Region, the Speaker and Deputy Speaker of the congress, and representatives of the Harari Region to the Council of Federation. In other words, members of the Harari ethnic group have assumed most of the important posts.

The Harari regional council, which comprises two houses, has the power to enact a constitution and laws for Harari region and amend the constitution. Since the Harari control a minimum of 14 seats out of the total 36, any law that is enacted in the region should be supported by them, especially those

---

[1] A traditional institution, historically a backbone of the Harari administration that keeps the land records and judges court cases according to the Sharia law.

[2] A traditional institution in Harari by which investigation is imposed upon a community for apprehending or identifying a wrongdoer.

laws that require a 2/3 of majority vote. No such right has been given to any other ethnic group in the region.

It was within this political climate and constitutional framework that the educational language policy was implemented during the last decade or so.

CHAPTER FOUR
THE ETHNOGRAPHY OF PRIMARY SCHOOLS IN HARARI: A CASE STUDY

This chapter describes the ethnography of elementary schools in Harari region by examining representative schools. It tries to give insight into the school environment and educational practices, the language use in the curriculum, classroom management and the 'entry' and 'exit' levels (as languages of instruction) of the three competing major languages of the region, namely Amharic, Harari and Oromo, as well as the international language, English. Before doing so, however, we shall first have a look at the general background of school performance in the region as indicated by school enrolment, dropout rates and repeaters in four consecutive years from 2000 to 2004 (Table 4.1).

4.1. Background

Primary school in the Harari Region and in Ethiopia in general is defined as consisting of grades one to–eight, and is divided into two cycles: first cycle is from grades one to four while the second cycle covers grades five to eight. In the Harari Region, which had a total population of 131,139 in 1994 and covers 314 sq. km. (CSA 1994), there are three high schools, one technical school, one Teacher Training Institute and 50 elementary schools, of which 24 are found in surrounding rural areas and the remaining 26 are urban-based schools located in the city of Harar. In this tiny and compact city-state, there are 19 urban and 17 rural *Kebeles*[3] as of 2005. On average there is more than one elementary school per kebele. Given the distribution and accessibility of schools in the region (one school within a 3 km radius in rural areas) the goal of universal primary education by 2015 seems to be attainable. The question, however, is whether all children, particularly girls and children belonging to ethnic minorities, in fact truly have access to free and compulsory primary education of good quality, as envisaged by the World Education Forum in Dakar, April 2000 (UNESCO 2002). A related issue is whether the use of vernaculars in the schools has really empowered minority groups by providing quality and equitable basic education as stated in the Millennium Development Goal of 'education for all' by 2015.

---

[3]Locality or lower level administrative unit within district in Ethiopia

Table 4.1. Enrolments, dropouts and repeaters (grades 1–8) for Harari Region in four consecutive years of 2000–2004

Academic Year	Area	Enrolments						Dropouts						Repeaters					
		M		F		Total		M		F		Total		M		F		Total	
		Fig	%	Fig	%	Fig		Fig	%	Fig	%	Fig	%	Fig	%	Fig	%	Fig	%
2000–2001	Urban	8425	52.2	7727	47.8	16152		555	6.6	618	8.0	1173	7.3	1254	14.9	1232	15.9	2486	15.4
	Rural	6852	69.3	3029	30.7	9881		1129	16.5	647	21.4	1776	18.0	553	8.1	235	7.8	788	8.0
	Total	**15277**	**58.7**	**10756**	**41.3**	**26033**		**1684**	**11.0**	**1265**	**11.8**	**2949**	**11.3**	**1807**	**11.8**	**1467**	**13.6**	**3274**	**12.6**
2001–2002	Urban	8909	53.9	7625	46.1	16534		914	10.3	597	7.8	1511	9.1	2105	23.6	1567	20.6	3672	22.2
	Rural	6689	69.4	2949	30.6	9638		1119	16.7	670	22.7	1789	18.6	947	14.2	412	14.0	1359	14.1
	Total	**15598**	**59.6**	**10574**	**40.4**	**26172**		**2033**	**13.0**	**1267**	**12.0**	**3300**	**12.6**	**3052**	**19.6**	**1979**	**18.7**	**5031**	**19.2**
2002–2003	Urban	10040	53.2	8823	46.8	18863		882	8.8	635	7.2	1517	8.0	1396	13.9	1258	14.3	2654	14.1
	Rural	6770	69.8	2931	30.2	9701		1606	23.7	650	22.2	2256	23.3	964	14.2	415	14.2	1379	14.2
	Total	**16810**	**58.9**	**11754**	**41.1**	**28564**		**2488**	**14.8**	**1285**	**10.9**	**3773**	**13.2**	**2360**	**14.0**	**1673**	**14.2**	**4033**	**14.1**
2003–2004	Urban	10252	53.5	8900	46.5	19152		924	9.0	664	7.5	1588	8.3	793	7.7	662	7.4	1455	7.6
	Rural	6471	68.1	3038	31.9	9509		1307	20.2	543	17.9	1850	19.5	538	8.3	224	7.4	762	8.0
	Total	**16723**	**58.3**	**11938**	**41.7**	**28661**		**2231**	**13.3**	**1207**	**10.1**	**3438**	**12.0**	**1331**	**8.0**	**886**	**7.4**	**2217**	**7.7**

SOURCE: Harari Regional Government Educational Bureau (2005)

According to the demographic data given in Table 4.1, the average mean for male dropouts was 13.02 per cent while it was 11.1 per cent for female dropouts. The average mean for rural dropouts in the four years, on the other hand, was 18.4 per cent while the average mean for urban dropouts was less than half of this, i.e. 8.1 per cent. Conversely, the rate of repeaters in the rural area was less than it was in the urban areas, the respective average means being 11 per cent and 14.15 per cent. The average mean of the repeaters in the four consecutive years was 12 per cent for males and 13.4 per cent for females.

Looking only at the first cycle, the dropout rate in rural schools was so high at average mean of 20.48 per cent (Table 4.2). There was no significant difference between dropout rates for male and female pupils; the average mean for male dropouts was 19.75 per cent while it was 20.4 per cent for female dropouts. The dropout rate in the third year (2002–2003) showed random fluctuation for male and female pupils, which was significantly higher than the dropout rate in the first two years; i.e. rate of male dropout was 24.3 per cent and female dropout was 23.2 per cent. During the fourth year, male dropouts decreased to 18.8 per cent and female dropouts to 18 per cent.

In rural areas the dropout rate was higher in the first cycle, the average mean being 20.1 per cent and lower in the second cycle, i.e. 17.8 per cent. Conversely, the average rate of repeaters in the second cycle (18.15 per cent) was over twice as high as the average rate of repeaters in the first cycle (8.4 per cent).

Table 4.2. Rate of enrolment, dropouts and repeaters in the first and second primary cycles in rural schools, in four consecutive academic years (2000–2004)

Year	School Performance	First Cycle (Grade 1-4) Pupil population by sex						Second Cycle (Grade 5-8) Pupil population by sex					
		M	%	F	%	Total	%	M	%	F	%	T	%
2000–2001	Enrolment	5156	65.5	2711	34.5	7867		1696	84.2	318	15.8	2014	
	Dropouts	937	18.2	611	22.5	1548	19.7	192	11.3	36	11.3	228	11.3
	Repeaters	386	7.5	210	7.7	596	7.6	167	9.8	25	7.9	192	9.5
2001–2002	Enrolment	4877	64.8	2654	35.2	7531		1812	86.0	295	14.0	2107	
	Dropouts	872	17.9	564	21.3	1436	19.1	247	13.6	106	35.9	353	16.8
	Repeaters	569	11.7	317	11.9	886	11.8	378	20.9	95	32.2	473	22.4
2002–2003	Enrolment	4592	65.0	2471	35.0	7063		2178	82.6	460	17.4	2638	
	Dropouts	1117	24.3	574	23.2	1691	23.9	489	22.5	76	16.5	565	21.4
	Repeaters	470	10.2	274	11.1	744	10.5	494	22.7	141	30.7	635	24.1
2003–2004	Enrolment	4337	63.6	2480	36.4	6817		2134	79.3	558	20.7	2692	
	Dropouts	817	18.8	447	18.0	1264	18.5	490	23.0	96	17.2	586	21.8
	Repeaters	197	4.5	113	4.6	310	4.5	341	16.0	111	19.9	452	16.8

SOURCE: Harari Regional Government Educational Bureau (2005)

Table 4.3. Rate of enrolment, dropouts and repeaters in the first and second primary cycles in urban schools, in four consecutive academic years (2000–2004)

Year	School Performance	First Cycle (Grade 1–4) Pupil population by sex						Second Cycle (Grade 5–8) Pupil population by sex					
		M	%	F	%	Total	%	M	%	F	%	T	%
	Enrolment	4183	**51.0**	4013	**49.0**	8196		4242	**54.5**	3544	**45.5**	7786	
2000–2001	Dropouts	277	6.6	235	5.9	512	6.2	278	6.6	383	10.8	**661**	8.5
	Repeaters	504	12.0	471	11.7	975	11.9	750	17.7	761	21.5	**1511**	19.4
	Enrolment	4321	**94.2**	4084	**89.0**	4588		4588	**56.4**	3541	**43.6**	**8129**	
2001–2002	Dropouts	436	10.1	372	9.1	808	17.6	478	10.4	225	6.4	**703**	8.6
	Repeaters	512	11.8	472	11.6	984	21.4	1218	26.5	1095	30.9	**2313**	28.5
	Enrolment	4633	**50.2**	4594	**49.8**	9227		5407	**56.1**	4229	**43.9**	**9636**	
2002–2003	Dropouts	360	7.8	365	7.9	725	7.9	522	9.7	270	6.4	**792**	8.2
	Repeaters	447	9.6	414	9.0	861	9.3	949	17.6	844	20.0	**1793**	18.6
	Enrolment	4812	**50.8**	4653	**49.2**	9465		5440	**56.2**	4247	**43.8**	**9687**	
2003–2004	Dropouts	391	8.1	356	7.7	747	7.9	533	9.8	308	7.3	**841**	8.7
	Repeaters	189	3.9	175	3.8	362	3.8	603	11.1	490	11.5	**1093**	11.3

SOURCE: Harari Regional Government Educational Bureau (2005)

In urban schools, the rate of repeaters in the first cycle (11.57 per cent) was less than the rate of repeaters in the second cycle (19.4 per cent) (Table 4.3). The dropout rate was slightly higher in the first cycle than in the second cycle; with respective average means of 9.85 per cent and 8.45 per cent. The dropout rate was similar in both rural and urban schools, being slightly higher in the first cycle. The rate of repeaters in both areas, on the other hand, is roughly twice as high in the second cycle as it is in the first cycle.

The general picture shows that the initial enrolment looks good but the overall rate of dropouts was reasonably high in second cycle/elementary schools, even twice as high in the rural schools as compared to in the urban schools. By contrast, the overall rate of repeaters was higher in urban schools than in rural schools. The number of repeaters was twice as high in the second cycle as compared to in the first cycle. So there is a clear correlation between dropout rates and the urban vs. rural dichotomy, on the one hand, and between rate of repeaters and first cycle/lower vs. Second cycle/upper primary education on the other (Table 4.4).

Table 4.4. The rate of repeaters and dropouts in rural and urban settings

	Repeaters		**Dropouts**	
	Rural	**Urban**	**Rural**	**Urban**
1st cycle	8.4	11.57	20.1	9.85
2nd cycle	18.5	19.4	17.8	8.45

SOURCE: Summarised from Harari Regional Government Educational Bureau (2005)

Part of the reason why there are dropouts and repeaters has been attributed to inaccessibility of the language that learners have to use in school (Romaine 1994). The question to be raised, in the context of Harari, is thus whether the policy implementation model adopted in a particular school has contributed to the success or failure of education using mother tongue as medium of instruction. To put it differently, in realizing the child's right to learn in his mother tongue, what practical steps have been taken towards the implementation of the multilingual educational policy? The following section describes the types of schools and school environments as well as logistic issues, as a prelude to discussion of the issues raised.

4.2. Typology of Schools and School Environments

4.2.1. Typology of Schools

Schools in Harari can be divided into heritage or native language schools, religious-based heritage schools, mainstream schools, and international schools (cf. Baker 1996 for a detailed typology of schools).

a) Heritage or Native Language Schools

Heritage or native language schools are numerically the majority in the region; they use either Harari or Oromo as medium of instruction for the first six years of elementary education. In many of these schools, Amharic is introduced at grade three, while English is given as a subject as of grade one and takes over as medium of instruction in grade seven. The ethos these schools are based upon is that children should use their native, ethnic, home or heritage language in the school as medium of instruction in order to achieve full bilingualism and bi-literacy. In the process, the child's native language is protected and developed alongside the development of the official language. Besides the pedagogical advantages of learning in the native or home language in the early stages, these schools are considered as fulfilling an important identity-forming and identity-preserving function for the minority communities, such as the Harari.

b) Religious-based Schools

In Harari, the religious-based school (there is only one) normally follows the pattern of heritage or native language schools but adds Arabic, a language given as a subject and also used as medium of religious study, with stress on Islamic traditions.

c) Mainstream Schools

Mainstream schools in Harari are only five in number and all are located in the city. They all use Amharic as medium of instruction for all subjects during the first six years, while English is given as a subject from grades one to eight. English replaces Amharic as medium of instruction as of grade seven. In these schools only two languages are used, i.e. the language of wider communication (LWC), Amharic, and the international language, English. This is the typical situation found in the capital Addis Ababa and in the Amhara Region, where Amharic is the dominant language. These mainstream schools have been retained from the previous system, when only mainstream schools were allowed, in order to address the needs of mixed multiethnic communities in the city of Harar. In some cases, there are two streams within the same school, such as in Ras Mekonnen Elementary School. One stream gives education in the LWC, i. e. Amharic, while the other stream teaches in the vernacular, Harari.

d) International Schools

The international school (again there is only one) is that of SOS, established in connection with a famine in the 1970s in order to help orphans.

Along these lines, six schools were selected for the purposes of this study based on the medium of instruction chosen to give basic education. Harari, Amharic, Oromo, Arabic and English are the languages used as media of instruction in the various schools. The schools chosen were:

1. Model I Elementary School (1–8 grades)—heritage language school where the medium of instruction is Oromo until grade six – an urban-based school;
2. Dire Teyara Elementary School (1–8 grades)—heritage language school where Oromo is the medium of instruction until grade six – a rural-based school;
3. Gey Medresa Elementary School (1–8 grades)—heritage language school where Harari is the medium of instruction from grade one to six;
4. Aw Abdal Elementary School (1–8 grades)—religious-based heritage language school where Harari is the medium of instruction and Arabic is a language given as a subject and also used as medium of instruction for religious studies;
5. Yeshimebet Elementary School (5–8 grades only)—mainstream school where the medium of instruction is solely Amharic for fifth and sixth grades; and
6. SOS Elementary and Secondary School (1–12 grades) —the medium of instruction is mainly English but supplemented by Amharic, which is used in the afternoon sessions as a reinforcement to teach the same subjects taught in English in the morning.

4.2.2. School Physical Environment

a) Model I Elementary School: A government school that was established in 1957 as a practice centre for training TTI (Teachers Training Institute) trainees. Since 1974, this has been changed and the school is independent of the TTI and operates as an elementary school (grade 1–8). Oromo is used as medium of instruction.

Model I has the typical look of most schools all over the country. It has two-storey G+1 buildings which are features of recent expansion and stand in sharp contrast to the older ground-floor buildings. There are also the grafitti on the walls, which are a point of commonality among most schools. The classrooms are also typical with an average of 50 pupils in each class. Since the classrooms are narrow and cramped, three or four pupils are seated at one desk, nudging and pushing each other as they try to make space for themselves.

When break time comes, the pupils seem grateful to be relieved from their overcrowded classrooms as they rush to the big, unkempt playground. Surrounded by tall trees, the shaded playground also provides welcome shelter from the midday sun. Standing near the classrooms, you look down on the red and yellow-clad children rushing around on the playground and feel like you are standing at the top of a hill looking at some animated capsules beneath you. Then, you realize that the school lies on very rugged terrain.

b) Dire Teyara Elementary School: After a seven-kilometre ride on dusty and bumpy roads outside of Harar, you get to an abandoned airstrip. Just to the left of this airstrip you find Dire Teyara (translates as 'Air strip') Elementary School, which handles more than 50 per cent of the educational needs of the area.

The dust-covered children with their dull-coloured uniforms welcome you as you enter the compound. You push through the crowd, careful not to trip over the children, and you are faced with the view of the school. There is nothing but red dust everywhere. It covers the plants, the classrooms and everything else. You know that by the time you leave, you too will look like a clay doll.

The classrooms are again narrow and dilapidated, the library is not furnished, there is no proper playground for the children, there are not enough toilets, etc. This reality clashes sharply with the fact that approximately 80 per cent of the families that send their children to this school are rich by most standards. Most parents are 'chat' farmers who distribute their products to exporters all over the country. So, why don't these people donate money to the school to make it more habitable than it is? The school administration thinks that these people do not really appreciate the value of education as such. They know that one can get rich without going to school, so they see no point in fostering a good environment for education. They send their children to school because the children need some place to spend the day. The children also are aware of their family's wealth and know that at some point in their life they will just quit their education and let their parents provide them with some capital to start up their own businesses or be involved in the family business. As a result, there is very little motivation to acquire knowledge.

Dire Teyara is a government school which was established around 1974. It now operates as an elementary school, using Oromo as medium of instruction.

c) Gey Medresa Elementary School: This school is located in the heart of the city of Harar, a city of mosques, markets and a centre of Islamic learning. Surrounded by the walls of Jegol, the city has its own unique culture and is regarded by most outsiders as a place of mystery and enchantment. It was founded during the 12th century and is now considered as a 'Holy City' by the Muslims (Harari National Regional State (ND)). Inside its walls are more than 90 mosques. Though predominantly a Muslim town, Harar also boasts an Orthodox Christian Church, the Church of *Medhane Alem*, or Saviour of the World. The year after the incorporation of Harar into the Ethiopian empire, i.e. 1888, Ras Mekonnen, the governor of Harar, built the church on the site of the principal mosque, which the Harari must have reckoned as their loss (Caulk 1971, 19). Today, however, one can see the coexistence of the two major religions side by side, reflecting the level of tolerance and the affable behaviour of the people of Harar. The building of an Orthodox Church at the heart of Jegol brought another religious language of Semitic origin, Ge'ez, onto the scene, adding to the complexity of the linguistic landscape of Harar.

All around the walled city and inside it are large and small markets, including the famous 'chat' market. You see quiet commotion as people go about their daily business. The school of Gey Medresa is situated inside this hubbub. . From every window of the classrooms, one can see the beauty of the ancient city. The old mosques, the old buildings, the old walls and the old alleyways all stand out in green and white splendour. The school merges inobtrusively into the ancient vista with its old buildings, on safety of which age has repercussions. As some of the teachers told us, the buildings are so old that the children are in danger.

Gey Medresa was started as a community-based school in 1932 by Sheh Abdulkerim in an attempt to protect the Harari language from being overrun by the Amharic-only policy of the time (cf. Chapter Three regarding the post-WWII period). The school was organized by the language community for its own survival. The school basically provided basic literacy in Amharic and religious education through Arabic. It also had a night school for volunteers who wanted to learn Harari, an act that defied the Haile Sellassie government's Amharic-only policy. During the Italian occupation, however, the use of Arabic was encouraged by the Italians, who had a policy of pitting different ethnic and religious groups against each other. This policy resonated with the Harari, who had been resentful of Christian domination (Carmichael 2001).

With the eruption of the popular revolution in 1974, which nationalized all private and public schools, Gey Medresa, like all other schools in the country, became a government school with Amharic as the sole medium of instruction. With the change of government in 1991, the school started teaching in three languages—Amharic, Oromo, and Harari—and turned a truly multilingual school with three media of instruction plus English as a subject. This was feasible because it was done in shifts. Instruction in Amharic was given from 6:00 a.m. to 10:00 a.m., instruction in Oromo from 10:30 a.m. to 2:00 p.m. and instruction in Harari from 2:30 p.m. to 5:50 p.m.; the shifts rotated every month. Each period constituted 35 minutes. This system continued for four years but could not be maintained because of the increasing number of pupils. As it could not be managed anymore, it was decided to make the medium of instruction only Harari. The rationales for maintaining only Harari as medium of instruction were: (1) the setting of the school is at the centre of Jegol, in the midst of the Harari-speaking community, and (2) the other groups, the Amhara and the Oromo, have alternative schools available right in the city of Harar.

Another interesting feature of the Gey Medresa School is the ethnic composition of the pupils. In 2005, the school had a total of 813 pupils, of whom 470 (57 per cent) were ethnically Harari, 210 (25 per cent) were Oromo, 113 (14 per cent) were Somali, 17 (two per cent) were Amhara and 3 (0.3 per cent) were who identified themselves as Arabs. More striking is that parents who had the option of sending their children to their respective ethnic schools opted for Harari. This is a situation where the linguistic composition of the school population has not always followed the lines of mother tongue education.

d) Aw Abdal Elementary School: the only religious-based school in Harar. This school was established around 1978. It was named after a certain Amir. It is now a community school with a total of 697 Muslim pupils.

The school lies on vast grounds, more than half of which are unused. You drive through the compound to get to where the administrative structure is situated in the middle of it. The classroom buildings are clustered around this structure as if sheltering it from harm. These buildings are comparatively recent and are rather far apart. Unlike many of the schools around, you do not see a big crowd of pupils. That may be because the school compound is very spacious and accommodates the density of the pupils well.

The brown and yellow-clad pupils greet you with cheerful, friendly smiles when you enter the school. To the dull and unattractive uniforms is added the ornamentation of the multi-coloured 'hijabs' the girls wrap around their heads. The 'hijab' resembles a sash. It is compulsory in the Muslim tradition for the women to cover their hair with this cloth. The monotonous uniforms are also relived by the bright smiles you get from the charming children. They talk to you with the most candid demeanour you have ever seen. They make you feel truly welcome in their own sincere way.

Apart from the religious orientation of the school, which makes it unlike the other schools described, there is one further remarkable difference. The number of female pupils is greater than that of the male pupils. Though this difference is not statistically significant, it is very visible to the observer. It is all the more noteworthy when one considers that the Muslim religion is basically male-dominated.

Another striking point is that the pupils attending this school have a very diverse ethnic composition, such as Oromo, Amhara, Harari, Arab, Gurage, and Tigrawi (Tigrinya-speaking). This ethnic diversity gives the school a certain zest for the outsider. The children are not self-conscious about their ethnic differences and befriend each other with no questions asked.

e) Yeshimebet Elementary School: The very narrow school compound is cluttered with buildings that have seen little renovation since they were first erected. You don't have to walk around much to discover what the school encompasses. Standing at the door you can witness what features make up the school.

There are drawings on the walls in bright colours proudly proclaiming the signatures of the pupils who painted them: a map of Africa, a map of Harar, the nine planets, all in huge distorted splendour testifying to the childish hands which painted them—an appreciable attempt to decorate what would otherwise be dreary surroundings. To the right, you can witness the sorry excuse for a playground, consisting of a swing hanging on a big tree. This is where the children are supposed to play.

The insides of the classrooms are dark for lack of windows that can bring in the sun's rays and are built like a narrow corridor. For this reason the pupils sit very close to each other. The average number of pupils in one class is 47, which, comparatively, is not too much. However, since the classrooms are so narrow, the number appears to be a crowd.

This school was established in 1944 and named after the mother of Emperor Haile Sellassie I. It was originally established as a school for girls but after the 1974 revolution, it started accepting also boys. It is now a school providing education for pupils from grades five to eight, accepting pupils who have completed grades one to four in another school (personal communication with the School Administration).

Given that Amharic serves as the medium of instruction until grade seven, one would assume the ethnic composition of the pupils to be comparatively uniform, constituting basically Amharas. However, there are also many Harari, Oromo, Somali, Gurage, Wolaytta and even Tigre-speaking pupils. It is especially noteworthy that Harari and Oromo families send their children to this school since they have the alternative of sending them to schools whose medium of instruction is their mother tongue.

f) SOS Elementary and Secondary School: The first SOS children's village was established in Imst, Austria in 1949. Its main objective was to provide a home for children orphaned during the Second World War. An Austrian benefactor named Herman Gemainer generated the idea. Countries all over the world took up the SOS initiative. There are now SOS villages in over 131 countries worldwide. In these countries, there are over 380 SOS villages with 40,000 children living in them (School brochure).

The first SOS children's village was established in Ethiopia in 1982. At the time, there was draught followed by famine in the northern parts of the country. The main victims of the catastrophe were children. So the SOS organization extended a helping hand and the first Ethiopian SOS village was established. The SOS villages expanded all over Ethiopia, giving much-needed help. The villages now incorporate service-giving facilities like schools and clinics that serve not only the village community but also the outside society. This is done so that the children will mix with the outside world. This helps to instil in them the feeling that they belong to the society at large and make them realize that they too are normal citizens.

There are now six SOS villages in various parts of Ethiopia (school brochure and personal communication with the school director). One is found in Harar. The Harar SOS village has elementary and secondary schools. The school is of international standard, both in syllabus and appearance. The school compound stands adjacent to the village. It covers a vast area, over which the classroom buildings are scattered comfortably.

The children have a playground with basketball courts, a football field and a gymnasium. There is also a cafeteria where they can have snacks at break time and lunch at their lunch hour. Everything is provided for the comfort of the children so that they can go about acquiring education contentedly.

4.3. Languages in the Curriculum

In talking about the role of languages in the curriculum, Bamgbose (1991, 62) notes that at least three major issues are involved: (1) which language to choose, (2) for what purpose, and (3) at what level. In any multilingual education programme that is launched in Harari region, the following choices present themselves concerning the language(s) to be used in the schools.

a) The child's mother tongue or vernacular (L1). The languages under this category are Harari and Oromo;

b) The language of wider communication (LWC) and the official working language of the Regional Government, Amharic (L2), which is also the official working language of the Federal government. This is an indigenous LWC used as a lingua franca and as an official/national language;

c) The language of higher education (both secondary and tertiary), which is an international language, English (L3); and

d) The language associated with Islam, i.e. classical Arabic (L4). Harar is considered a 'holy city' by Muslims, and the dominance of Islam is readily visible. Arabic is an international language that has been used for literacy and religious teachings for centuries; its function in Harar, however, is rather restricted.

The introduction of one or more of these languages, the roles assigned to them, and the level at which they are introduced depend on the type of school, the objectives of that particular school, the ideology of the power structure and the ethnic group the language is associated with.

In Harari, the Oromo, Harari, Amharic, English and Arabic languages are all used for conducting literacy, i.e. initial literacy for children, and are given as a subject and also used as media of instruction for other subjects. Except for English, which replaces all the vernaculars at grade seven, these languages are all used at primary level with the aim of providing basic education.

The use of languages in the curriculum for Harari region is in line with the international approach to the problem of multilingual education advocated by UNESCO (2003) and other educationalists. The UNESCO position particularly recommends a well-structured approach to multilingual education by introducing three languages, i.e. the mother tongue (MT-L1), the regional or national language (L2), and an international language (L3). The rationale for introducing three languages was stated in the 2003 position paper entitled "Education in a multilingual world" (p. 26) as follows:

1) mother tongue instruction at the beginning of formal education for pedagogical, social and cultural considerations;
2) multilingual education with a view to the preservation of cultural identities; and
3) foreign language learning as part of an intercultural education aiming at the promotion of understanding between communities and between nations.

The following section presents description of the role of the mother tongues (L1), the LWC (L2) and the foreign languages (L3 and L4) in the sample schools in Harari region, and the function of each language in the curriculum as well as the time allocated to each language. Then it discusses the implementation models of each school and sees if the role played by each language in the curriculum is in line with the international standard proposed by UNESCO and other educationalists.

a) Model I Elementary School: Oromo is the medium of instruction; English is introduced as a subject in the first grade and continues to be given as a subject until the seventh grade, at which point it becomes the medium of instruction. Also Amharic is given as a subject from grade three to grade eight. English and the mother tongue, Oromo, are introduced simultaneously at grade one and continue to be given as a subject throughout elementary education (see Table 4.5).

Table 4.5. Languages in the curriculum in the Model I Elementary School

Type of school	Languages	1	2	3	4	5	6	7*	8*
Oromo	Oromo	O	O	O	O	O	O	o/O**	o/O**
Heritage	Amharic			a	a	a	a	a	A
School	English	e	e	e	e	e	e	E	E

* In grades 7 & 8, social studies and civic education are given in Oromo while other subjects are taught in English.
Capital letters E, O, and A indicate the level at which Harari, English, Oromo and Amharic, respectively, are used as a medium of instruction and taught as a subject, while the corresponding lowercase letters **h, e, o, and **a** stand for the level at which the languages are taught only as a subject.

However, the time allocation for the three languages (Oromo, English, and Amharic) differs from one grade to the other. Oromo is given for five periods per week for grades one to four, four periods per week for grades five and six, and three periods per week for grades seven and eight. English is given five periods per week for all grade levels. Amharic is given five periods per week for grades three and four, four periods per week for grades five and six, and three periods per week for grades seven and eight. Except for English, the time allocated for the other languages decreases as the grade level increases (Table 4.6). This is partly because new subjects, such as chemistry and physics, are introduced in grades seven and eight. However, even after grade seven, social studies and civic education are given in Oromo. After grade seven, therefore, there is language separation by subject, i.e. different subjects are allocated to different languages.

Table 4.6. Language allocation within classroom in Model I School

No. of periods per week	Languages and corresponding grade levels		
	Oromo	Amharic	English
5	1–4th	3–4th	1–8th
4	5–6th	5–6th	—
3	7–8th	7–8th	—

b) Dire Teyara Elementary School: Likewise, in all subjects are given in Oromo until grade seven, at which time the medium of instruction changes to English. English is given as a subject staring from grade one until it becomes the medium of instruction. Amharic comes on the scene in grade three and continues to be given as a subject through grade eight (Table 4.7).

Table 4.7. Languages in the curriculum in Dire Teyara Elementary School

Type of school	Languages	Level							
		1	2	3	4	5	6	7	8
Oromo Heritage School	Oromo	O	O	O	O	O	O	o/O*	o/O*
	Amharic			a	a	a	a	a	A
	English	e	e	e	e	e	e	E	E

* In grades 7 and 8, social studies and civic education are given in Oromo while other subjects are taught in English.

The time allocated for Oromo is five periods per week for grades one to four, and two periods per week for grades five to eight. Amharic is given three periods per week for grades three to seven and four periods per week for grade eight. The time allocated for English is uniform from grade one to eight, that is five periods per week (Table 4.8).

Table 4.8. Language allocation within classroom in Dire Teyara School

No. of periods per week	Languages and corresponding grade levels		
	Oromo	Amharic	English
5	1–4ᵗʰ	—	1–8ᵗʰ
4	—	8th	—
3	—	3–7ᵗʰ	—
2	5–8ᵗʰ	—	—

c) Gey Medresa Elementary School: Starting in the year 1995 the medium of instruction became the Harari language. Amharic and English are introduced simultaneously in grade one. After grade seven, while English becomes the medium of instruction for most subjects, the vernacular is reserved for music and sport (Table 4.9). Here again the language separation in classrooms is done by subject.

Table 4.9. Languages in the curriculum in Gey Medresa Elementary School

Type of school	Languages	Level							
		1	2	3	4	5	6	7	8
Harari Heritage School	Harari	H	H	H	H	H	H	h/H*	h/H*
	Amharic	a	a	a	a	a	a	a	a
	English	e	e	e	e	e	e	E	E

* In grades 7 and 8, music and sport are given in Harari while other subjects are taught in English.

Amharic is given for three periods per week for all grade levels; English five periods per week for grades one to four; six periods per week for grades five and six; and again five periods per week for grades seven and eight; while Harari is given four periods a week for grades one to six; and three periods per week for grades seven and eight (Table 4.10). Harari is the mother tongue of almost all the pupils attending the school.

Table 4.10. Language allocation within classroom in Gey Medresa School

No. of periods per week	Languages and corresponding grade levels		
	Harari	Amharic	English
6	—	—	5–6th
5	—	—	1–4ᵗʰ ; 7–8th
4	1–6th	—	—
3	7–8ᵗʰ	1–8th	—

d) Aw Abdal Elementary School: uses Harari as the medium of instruction with Amharic, English and Arabic given as subjects. Amharic is introduced at the third grade while Arabic and English are introduced at the first grade (Table 4.11).

Table 4.11. Languages in the curriculum in the religious-based Aw Abdal Elementary School

Languages	Level							
	1	2	3	4	5	6	7	8
Harari	H	H	H	H	H	H	h/H*	h/H*
Amharic			am	am	am	am	am	am
English	e	e	e	e	e	e	E	E
Arabic	ar/A*	ar/A*	ar/A*	ar/A*	ar/ A*	ar/ A*	ar/ A*	ar/ A*

* In grades 7 and 8 music and sport are given in Harari while other subjects are taught in English. Arabic is the medium for religious education in all grades.

Harari is given five periods a week for grades one to four; four periods a week for grades five and six; and three periods a week for grades seven and eight. Arabic is given five periods a week for grades one to four; four periods a week for grades five and six; and three periods a week for grades seven and eight. Amharic is given five periods a week for grades three and four; four periods a week for grades five and six; and two periods a week for grades seven and eight. English is given six periods a week for grades one to six and five periods a week for grades seven and eight (Table 4.12).

Table 4.12. Language allocation within classroom in Aw Abdal School

No. of periods per week	Languages and corresponding grade levels			
	Harari	*Amharic*	*English*	*Arabic*
6	—	—	1–6th	—
5	1–4th	3–4th	7–8th	1–4th
4	5–6th	5–6th	—	5–6th
3	7–8th	—	—	7–8th
2	—	7–8th	—	—

In Aw Abdal, the time allocation for the four languages as subjects takes up half of the total time allocated for all subjects. The emphasis given to language classes must have caused some time constraint in the curriculum, as it is a heavy language programme.

e) *Yeshimebet Elementary School (grades 5–8 only)* uses Amharic as medium of instruction until the pupils reach grade seven (Table 4.13). Starting from grade seven, Amharic is given as a subject for five periods a week. English is given as a subject for grades five and six for six periods per week until in grade seven (Table 4.14). From grade seven on, English becomes the medium of instruction for all subjects except civic education, which continues to be given in Amharic. Different curriculum areas are taught in different languages so that the school system follows a dual language approach at the higher elementary grades.

Table 4.13. Languages in the curriculum in Yeshimebet Elementary School (Grades 5-8 only)

Type of school	Languages	Level 5	6	7	8
Main Stream School	Amharic	A	A	a/A*	a/A*
	English	e	e	E	E

* In grades 7 & 8 civic education is taught in Amharic while other subjects are given in English

Table 4.14. Language allocation within classroom at Yeshimebet Elementary School (Grades 5-8 only)

No. of periods per week	Languages and corresponding grade levels	
	Amharic	*English*
6	—	5–6th
5	5–8th	7–8th

f) The SOS International School uses English as a medium of instruction at all grade levels. All the subjects given in English in the morning are repeated in Amharic during afternoon classes for the purpose of reinforcement and reviewing of concepts. However, here there is a danger of duplication of content: when the same subject matter is repeated in a different language, some pupils may be bored and not be able to concentrate. In any case, the strategy used in language allocation is to operate at different times in different languages. The morning courses are taught in English and the afternoon courses in Amharic. Strategies of separating, allocating or integrating the two languages in the classroom have not been seriously considered because the SOS international school is obliged by the regulations of the Ministry of Education to include Amharic in its curriculum. As of grade seven, the system changes in that all subjects are given in English except Amharic which continues to be given as a subject.

From grade 1–6, subjects given in the morning in English (5 periods a week) are repeated in Amharic (3 periods a week) in the afternoon. The time allocation is 62.5 per cent for English and 37.5 per cent for Amharic.

English is given seven periods per week while Amharic is given five periods per week at all grade levels. As of seventh grade, Amharic is given only as a subject. Moreover, the school follows a dual system using both English and Amharic. For instance, science subjects are taught five periods per week in English during the morning sessions and three times a week in Amharic in the afternoon sessions. Time allocation reflects the importance given to a subject in the curriculum. The prime teaching periods in the morning go to teaching in English while the afternoon is allocated for teaching in Amharic.

4.4. Implementation Models

The implementation models adopted in primary education in the Harari region are summarized in Table 4.15.

Table 4.15. Summary of the implementation models adopted in the various schools

Languages				L E V E L				
	1	2	3	4	5	6	7	8
Harari	H*	H	H	H	H	H	h/H[1]	h/H[1]
Oromo	O*	O	O	O	O	O	o/O[2]	o/O[2]
Amharic (Type 1)	am	am	am	am	am	am	am/AM[3]	am/AM[3]
Amharic (Type 2)	–	–	am	am	am	am	am/AM[3]	am/AM[3]
Amharic (Type 3)	AM*	AM	AM	AM	AM	AM	Am/AM[3]	Am/AM[3]
Amharic (Type 4)	AM	AM	AM	AM	AM	AM	am	am
English (Type 1)	e	e	e	e	e	e	E	E
English (Type 2)	E*	E	E	E	E	E	E	E
Arabic	ar/A[4]	ar/A[4]	ar/A[4]	ar/A[4]	ar/A[4]	ar/A[4]	ar/A[4]	ar/A[4]

* Capital letters H, O, AM, and E indicate the level at which Harari, Oromo, Amharic and English, respectively, are used as a medium of instruction and taught as a subject, while the corresponding lowercase letters h, o, am, e and ar stand for the level at which the languages are taught only as a subject.

[1] In grades 7 and 8 music and sport are given in Harari while other subjects are taught in English.
[2] In grades 7 and 8 social studies and civic education are given in Oromo while other subjects are taught in English.
[3] In grades 7 and 8 civic education is taught in Amharic while other subjects are given in English.
[4] Arabic is used as medium of instruction for religious teaching in all grades.

As shown in Table 4.15, the vernaculars Harari (H) and Oromo (O) serve as media of instruction up to grade six. In grades 7 and 8 both languages continue to be media of instruction for certain subjects, such as music, sports, social studies and civic education, with some variations from one school to the other. The use of Amharic in the curriculum is the most inconsistent. Type 1 (am) is where Amharic is given as a subject from grade one until grade six. Type 2 (am) is a model that introduces Amharic at grade three and gives it as a subject until grade six. Type 3 (AM) uses Amharic as a medium of instruction until grade six. In these schools, Amharic continues to be given as a subject and is retained as a medium of instruction for some subjects, such as civic education in upper elementary/second cycle primary level. This is the typical case in mainstream schools. Type 4 (AM) is where Amharic is used as a medium of instruction from grade one parallel with English. Amharic is used in the afternoon to teach the same subjects taught in English in the morning sessions but for fewer periods. In one type of curriculum, English (e) is given as a subject as of grade one and becomes the medium of instruction as of grade seven. This is the pattern in most schools, both government and private. The second type is where English (E) is the medium of instruction as of grade one all the way through elementary education, a case typical of international schools. Arabic (ar) is given in a religious-based school as a subject from grade one to the end of primary education. It is also used as medium of instruction for religious teaching.

The first feature of the various multilingual implementation models is that they clearly involve the use of at least three languages. Harari and Oromo are mother tongues (L1) and Amharic is an indigenous LWC (L2). English and Arabic are foreign languages, (L3). These models are in line with UNESCO's recommendation to have three languages (L1, L2 and L3) in multilingual primary education; an assumption that follows from the position that teaching in the mother tongue is most effective in the academic achievement and cognitive development of the child. The models implemented in Harari have, therefore, a strong component of mother tongue education since they use multiple languages at the lower (first cycle) and upper (second cycle) primary education and teach the languages as a subject throughout the elementary education system.

The second feature of the models is the lack of any coherent and consolidated policy towards the use of LWC, i.e. Amharic in the curriculum. The use of Amharic as a medium of instruction and the time allocation for the teaching of Amharic as a subject shows great inconsistency. This absence of a steady policy towards Amharic, as opposed to English, reflects the ideological stance of the political structure. Relatively, the use of English is consistent and there is a uniform policy and practice in the school system. Yet, Amharic serves as the official working language of the regional and the federal government and as a lingua franca for the various ethnic groups residing in Harar. Besides its political and psychological dominance, Amharic has a well-developed literature which provides access to a much wider store of knowledge than can be provided by an indigenous language. Pupils who do not go beyond the first cycle will be cut off from the LWC and the benefits that will accrue from the knowledge of Amharic. Note that the dropout rate in the region in the first cycle, i.e. grades 1–4, was between 18 and 23 per cent in the years 2000–2004 (see Tables 4.2 and 4.3 in the preceding pages of this chapter). Since these children will have left school before they master the LWC or the lingua franca of the region as well as the country, it will be very difficult for them to operate in a linguistic environment they are unfamiliar with (see Mchazine 2003, 22) for a similar observation). This pressing need for the promotion of literacy in the LWC has not been recognized by the political system of the region.

This leads us to another important issue in language policy, i.e. whether the policy is inherently unequal and denies equitable access to and achievement in basic education and respects the linguistic rights of the child. As rightly pointed out by Skutnabb-Kangas and Philipson (1995), as much as a child has the right to learn in his/her mother tongue, he/she also has the linguistic right to learn the official language of the country.

Yet another outstanding feature of the models is the entry and exit levels of the languages as languages of instruction in the curriculum. The entry level for the two international languages, English and Arabic, as well as the two vernacular languages, Oromo and Harari, is grade one. By contrast, the entry level for Amharic, the LWC, varies from school to school. In some of the schools where Harari is the medium, Amharic is taught as of grade one along with English and Arabic. In schools where Oromo is the medium of instruction, Amharic starts at grade three. On the other hand, the exit level for Amharic, Oromo and Harari is uniform in all the schools. At grade seven all are replaced, for most subjects, by English, which serves as the medium of instruction all the way through the tertiary level.

In terms of time allocation of each language in the classroom, a wide range of patterns has been observed even between schools using the same medium of instruction. For instance, in Model I School, Oromo is given five periods a week in the lower classes (1–4), four periods a week for grades five and six and three periods a week for seventh and eighth grades. In Dire Teyara, on the other hand, Oromo is taught for five periods a week in the first cycle (1–4th grades) and two periods a week in the second cycle (5–8th grades). Harari is taught in Aw Abdal School for five periods per week in the lower classes (1–4th grades), four periods a week in grades five and six, and three periods a week in the upper classes (7–8th grades). In Gey Medresa the pattern is different: Harari is given for four periods per week from grade one to six and three periods per week for grades seven and eight. A similar lack of uniformity applies to Amharic and English as well. The emphasis on this language or that seems to depend on the local interests of a particular school. Once again, lack of consistency in language allocation in classrooms and the consequent disparity of competence in the major languages among pupils constitute another pitfall of the implementation models.

The right of an individual child to use the language of his or her own choice is entrenched in the 1994 Language and Training Policy of the Ministry of Education. In contrast to other regions, this option is concretely available to children in the Harari region. Parents have the right to choose the school of their preference and to exercise language rights on behalf of their children while they are minors. It has been observed that the choice of the parents is not always dictated by the medium of instruction the school uses. As pointed out earlier, the often multi-ethnic composition of the pupils, especially in heritage schools, shows that the language of the school is not the only factor that influences the choice of parents. There are a multitude of reasons for this (see Chapter Five on the attitudes of parents). Some parents send their children to a school where the children will be exposed to a language other than their own. For instance, some Harari children are sent to mainstream schools where the LWC, Amharic, is the medium of instruction. Children from the various ethnic groups are also sent to the international school, SOS, where the medium is English supplemented by Amharic. This could plausibly reflect parents' be due to the aspirations to upward mobility for their children so that they may have a better future. A good many children from the Oromo and Amhara ethnic groups, on the other hand, are sent to heritage schools, such as Gey Medresa and Aw Adbal schools, perhaps due to the Islamic affiliation of these schools. Thus, children may end up in mainstream or heritage school despite their ethnic origin or mother tongue for any of a multitude of reasons.

The freedom of choice and opportunity has led to the wide range of implementation models presented earlier. It cannot be expected that a single uniform implementation model would or could lead to satisfactory results in such a diverse multiethnic polity.

4.5. Classroom Management

One noticeable feature observed in the heritage schools in particular is that, although the native or home language is used in the classroom, at times school management is conducted in the LWC, Amharic. Posters, announcements and charts are mostly in Amharic. In some cases, the multilingual nature of the schools is not at all evident from the way notices are posted inside and outside the buildings. Arguably, the school environment should better reflect the commitment of the school community to the goal of promoting multilingualism. For effective multilingual education, there is a need to encourage native language skills even outside the formal curriculum, in order to actively integrate aspects of pupil's home culture and values into the classroom.

Like most other government schools in the region, the Harari schools operate under the government policy called the "self-contained" programme. This programme involves free promotion of pupils with continuous assessment from grades one to four. One teacher teaches all subjects and guides a section throughout. Evaluation is both academic and non-academic. Everything, including the personal hygiene of the pupils, gets inspected.

In two heritage schools, Model I and Dire Teyara, where the medium is Oromo, as well as in the mainstream school, the absolute number of pupils decreases in upper primary grades. The reason for this perceptible drop in the number of pupils is that the practice of free promotion is abandoned after grade four; pupils are promoted only if they pass exams. Since there is the likelihood of large numbers of pupils failing exams, the number of pupils decreases as one goes up the grades. This explains why the rate of repeaters is so high in the second cycle (see Tables 4.2 and 4.3).

One serious problem associated with the implementation of the self-contained teaching method is the very large number of pupils in one class. In the lower primary classes, classrooms are jam-packed, sometimes with four to five pupils sitting at one desk. For instance, in Dire Teyara there are, on average, 70 pupils in one classroom. For one teacher to evaluate and follow up on each and every pupil in the class is virtually impossible. Another problem is that the policy was started only fairly recently and there is shortage of teachers trained to teach under the self-contained programme. The administration has suggested some solutions for these problems, such as splitting the load between teachers, increasing the number of teachers assigned to the school, and as a last resort, limiting the number of pupils accepted every year. Thus, the policy of making every primary teacher to teach all subjects including English and the vernacular language in the situation of overcrowded classes has proved to be ineffective.

On the other hand, in Gey Medresa and Aw Abdal Schools, where Harari is the medium, the average number in a classroom is 36 and 40 respectively. The much lower number of pupils in each class reflects clearly upon classroom management. It is less difficult for the teachers to handle and evaluate the pupils properly. The pupils also get to sit comfortably and have adequate space to move about.

In a typical international school, SOS, the average number of pupils in one class is not more than 30 and the teachers manage the classroom very easily. The objective of the SOS to provide a comfortable environment and standard education for the children seems to be a smashing success, since every year the high school graduates almost all of its pupils with almost no dropouts or failures.

One interesting aspect of classroom management in all the schools is the involvement of parental committees in maintaining discipline and the smooth running of classroom activities. The cooperation of parents with the school administrations was exemplary. Parents were encouraged to become involved in their children's education.

We witnessed one very good example while we were visiting Dire Teyara School. When one pupil showed bad discipline toward his teacher, the parental committee, all men, convened to decide what sort of punishment the pupil should receive. They gathered under the shade of a tree and took out bundles of 'chat' and started chewing before they started discussing the matter. It was as if they were heating up their engines before plunging into their task of shaping one pupil's fate.

Similarly, in a mainstream school, i.e. in Yeshimebet Elementary School, we observed an impressive collaboration between the school administration and the community. There is a strong sense of teamwork exhibited between the parental committee, the disciplinary committee, and the administration. Everything, from minor disciplinary problems of pupils to serious misconduct by the teachers, passes through the scrupulous investigation of the disciplinary committee working hand in hand with the parental and administrative group. In attending to molehills before they become mountains, the school administration hopes to bring into society a better generation.

In summary, the multilingual vernacular education in Harari has the following features.

(1) Parents have the choice of which school to send their children to. The system gives freedom of choice in selecting schools, unlike any other region in the country. In other parts of Ethiopia, there is only one choice, either the mainstream school or the heritage language school; in some cases, such as in the capital Addis Ababa there is a second choice, an international school, but it is not accessible to the majority.

(2) There are also situations where more than one language is adopted as a medium of instruction: English and Amharic in an international school, such as SOS; and Amharic and Harari in a mainstream school, such as Ras Mekonnen Elementary School (not one of the six considered in this study). Complementary media of instruction, involving the teaching of some subjects in L1 (mother tongue) and some in L3 (international language) in the upper primary, is a feature of some of the implementation models.

(3) All heritage schools are elementary schools; the exit level for Harari and Oromo, the two vernaculars used as media of instruction, is seventh grade.

(4) Bi-literacy and bilingualism are the objective, with literacy being acquired in both the native and English languages either simultaneously or with an initial emphasis on native language literacy. Use of L1 as a medium in lower and upper primary classes, ultimately giving way to L3 (English), seems to enhance cultural

enrichment through a broadening of knowledge to include that available in L3, in this case English (Bamgbose 1991,74);

(5) The entry level for international languages, such as English and Arabic is grade one. The entry level for Amharic, the language of wider communication and the official language of the region, lacks uniformity. The implementation model favours international languages over the official working language of the region. One of the shortcomings of the policy is, therefore, the teaching of the official language of the country. Given the lack of uniformity in the teaching of LWC, the policy has no mechanism to ensure that inconsistencies in mastering the official-national language will be minimized, let alone eliminated.

(6) The "self-contained teaching method" is the official policy of schools for the first cycle. This is a teaching method in which one teacher is required to teach all subjects, including English and the vernacular, and guides the section throughout and in all subjects. As explained, under the circumstances this has proved to be an ill-advised teaching method.

(7) In an attempt to rectify the problems related to standardization and language development, the "Harari Language Academy" has recently been formed (2005). The Academy has been commissioned to develop, modernize and standardize the Harari language; it is accountable to the regional parliament and may initiate legislation, policy and practice dealing with language. This is a significant step forward in recognizing the need to develop and standardize the vernacular for modern use and forming a responsible body, instead of proceeding in a haphazard and amateurish way, as has been the case in many regions in the country. The formulation of a language policy and its implementation are continuous processes that require revision from time to time depending on the changes on the ground. Although there are other major and competing languages in the region, such as Oromo and Amharic, the Academy was formed exclusively for the use and promotion of the Harari language.

As pointed out at the beginning of this chapter, the overall aim of the multilingual education programme launched in Harari as well as elsewhere in Ethiopia is to empower minority groups by providing quality and equitable education. Cummins (1986) quoted in Baker (1996, 346), in his psycholinguistic model called the 'Interdependency hypothesis', suggests that minority language pupils are 'empowered' or 'disabled' by four characteristics of schools. Three of the characteristics most relevant to our discussion are the following.

(1) ***Additive vs. subtractive dimension:*** This is the extent to which the home language and culture are incorporated into the school curriculum. Baker (1996, 346) stresses, "If a minority language child's home language

and culture are excluded, minimized or quickly reduced in school the likelihood is there of that child becoming academically 'disabled'. Where the school incorporates, encourages and gives status to the minority language, the chances of empowerment are increased".

(2) *Collaborative vs. exclusionary dimension:* This dimension has to do with the extent to which minority communities are encouraged to participate in their children's education.

(3) *Reciprocal interaction vs. transmission oriented curriculum:* This has to do with the extent to which education promotes the inner desire of children to become active seekers of knowledge and not just passive receptacles.

As shown in the preceding discussion, the system now in place in Harari is a form of additive multilingual education that has incorporated vernaculars and given status to minority languages. Furthermore, community participation has been collaborative, as seen in the parental committees making important decisions regarding school life as a whole. The nature of the curriculum and its impact on minority language pupils is discussed in Chapter Seven.

CHAPTER FIVE

LANGUAGE USE, ATTITUDES AND PATTERNS OF MULTILINGUALISM

5.1. Introduction

This chapter stands out from others in that it presents the findings from the quantitative component of the study. It discusses the language use situations and the nature of multilingualism in Harari. It also assesses the attitudes of pupils, parents and teachers on a wide range of issues, such as the choice and utility of medium of instruction (MOI) in schools, the use of mother tongue (MT) and the use of the language of wider communication (LWC) in primary education. Attitudes towards the capabilities of MT, attitudes towards the appropriateness of the scripts adopted and the use of other competing languages in the region will be explored.

5.2. Research Instruments

Prior to embarking on the main study, a pilot study was carried out in the city of Harar by selecting a limited number of respondents and administering the questionnaires to them. The objective of this pilot study was to test the questionnaires before the main study was conducted and hence to increase the validity of the study.

The pilot survey was made at four selected schools which use different media of instruction. They were: Model 1 Elementary School (1–8 grades) with Oromo being the medium of instruction; SOS Elementary and Secondary School where the MOI is English and Amharic; Gey Medresa Elementary School (1–8 grades) where the MOI is Harari; and Yeshimebet Elementary School (5–8 grades) with Amharic being the MOI.

For the pilot survey, altogether 171 questionnaires were administered in the four schools. Of these, 61 subjects were teachers and the remaining 110 were pupils of grade five. Pupils of grade five were selected for the pilot survey on the following basis.

a) In the Ethiopian school system primary education is divided into two cycles: a first cycle comprises grades 1–4 and a second cycle comprising grades 5–8. The fifth grade pupils are those who are just starting the second cycle; and

b) As graduates of the first cycle, fifth graders are expected to be literate – to have acquired basic skills in reading, writing and arithmetic. Since one of the objectives of this study was to evaluate the implementation of the educational policy and its results, choosing fifth grade pupils as a target was considered appropriate. In terms of age and maturity, it was also more convenient to administer questionnaires and interviews with grade five pupils than with lower graders.

Some insights were gained from the pilot study. For instance, the questionnaires should have been translated into Oromo for the Model 1 primary school where the medium is Oromo. Most pupils found it difficult to understand the questionnaires prepared in Amharic, the LWC. For SOS Primary and Secondary school, where the medium is English, many of the questions related to "mother tongue" became irrelevant since there are no mother tongue speakers of English in that school. This fact suggested that a modified version of the questionnaires should have been prepared for this particular school to make the questions relevant to the situation of the respondents. Some vague and ambiguous questions that respondents failed to understand were corrected. A few were omitted and new ones were added.

Based on the revised questionnaires, all the questions and the possible responses were coded and keyed into the computer for analysis using the SPSS. The questionnaires were translated into Oromo for Model I and Dire Teyara Elementary Schools, two of the schools selected for the study, where the medium is Oromo. The revised questionnaires were translated in order to overcome the language barrier that was encountered during the pilot study in administering the original questionnaires.

The questionnaire for the pupils has four parts. Part one contains basic information on the area of the study and has nine items. Part two focuses on the pupil's background and has 16 items. Part three has 10 items that deal with language attitude and part four has 10 items that deal with mother tongue education.

The second questionnaire, which was designed for assessing the attitudes and beliefs of parents, has three parts. Part one contains 13 questions of basic information; part two focuses on background information of the respondents and has 12 items; and part three has attitude questions, which comprise 14 items.

The third questionnaire was designed for teachers with the aim of assessing their attitudes and beliefs on the use of local languages in the curriculum. This questionnaire also has four parts. The first part has seven items that deal with basic information. The second deals with the background information of the respondents and has 16 items. The third section, which also has 16 items, focuses on the attitude of teachers towards mother tongue education; and the fourth section, which has 22 items, asks about the problems the mother tongue education has encountered, in their respective schools, and the inputs available to implement mother tongue education.

5.3. Characteristics of Respondents

5.3.1. Pupils

Age: As indicated in Chapter One, the number of pupils interviewed in the six schools was 678. The sample shows that the respondents were between the age of 8 and 16, and the average mean was 11.8 per cent. The majority (26.5 per cent) were 13 years of age; the second largest (19.2 per cent) were 11 years of age; and the third and fourth largest were 10 and 12 years old respectively. Age distribution by school shows that in the international school, the oldest pupil was 13 years of age. In Model I school, pupils above the age of 13 years constituted 20.8 per cent, in Dire Teyara10.5 per cent, in Gey Medresa 21.7 per cent and in the mainstream (Yeshimebet) school10.9 per cent.

Sex: In some schools, the proportion of female pupils exceeded the males; in some other schools the proportion was vice versa, and in some the sexes were equally balanced. The case where female pupils exceeded the males is interesting since this pattern deviates from the general trend in the country. In the schools where Harari was used as the medium of instruction, the number of female pupils was much greater than the male pupils. For instance, in Aw Abdal Elementary School, a religious-based school affiliated to Islam, 73.5 per cent were female pupils while only 26.5 per cent were male. Similarly, in Gey Medresa elementary school, 55.8 per cent were female pupils and 41.7 per cent were male pupils.

Generally, across all the schools, the proportion of male and female pupils was almost equal, which is not the case in other regional states. Male pupils in Harari region constituted 48.4 per cent and female pupils 48.7 per cent (the other 2.9 per cent did not indicate their sex). In the samples taken from a mainstream school, for example in Yeshimebet Elementary School, female pupils were 47.1 per cent and male pupils were 51.3 per cent. In Model I Elementary School, where the MOI is Oromo, the distribution of female and male pupils was almost equal: both constituted 47.5 per cent; the remaining 5 per cent did not indicate their sex. In a rural school, Dire Teyara, on the other hand, the number of male pupils was much greater (61.8 per cent) than the number of female pupils (30.9 Per cent) (Figure 5.1).

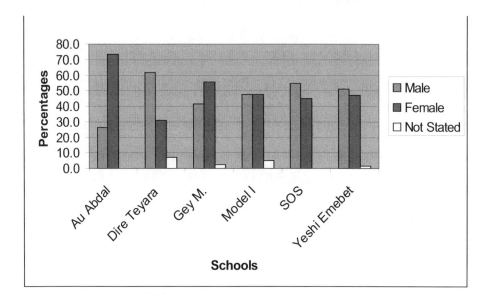

Figure 5.1. Respondents Distribution by Sex and by School

Ethnic Groups: Generally, 45.7 per cent of the total respondents identified themselves as Oromo; 24.2 per cent as Amhara and 18 per cent as belonging to the Harari ethnic group. In addition to these three major groups, the sample also included three minority groups, namely, Gurage (4 per cent), Tigrawi (2.5 per cent), and Somali 2.2 (per cent). There were also other minorities which constituted 2.5 per cent of the total sample, and a few foreign nationals (Arabs) which accounted for 0.9 per cent.

Looking into the distribution of ethnicity by school, however, gives a different picture. There is a correlation between the medium of instruction of the school and the dominant ethnic group in the school. In schools where Harari was the medium, such as Aw Abdal and Gey Medresa, the majority of the pupils, that is 61.4 per cent in Aw Abdal and 45 per cent in Gey Medresa, were of the Harari ethnic group. The second largest group in both schools was Oromo, consisting of 20.5 per cent in Aw Abdal and 32.5 per cent in Gey Medresa schools. The number of ethnically Gurage and Somali in both schools is quite significant. The Gurage constituted 4.8 per cent in Aw Abdal and 6.7 per cent in Gey Medresa schools; and the Somali groups constituted 4.8 per cent in Aw Abdal and 5.8 per cent in Gey Medresa School.

As discussed in Chapter Four (Section 4.2), the demographic profile of the entire population of the Gey Medresa school showed that 57 per cent were Harari; 25 per cent were Oromo; 14 per cent were Somali; and 2 per cent were Amhara. On the contrary, in schools where Oromo was the medium of instruction, such as Dire Teyara (rural school), 98.4 per cent of the respondents were of the Oromo ethnic group and the remaining were from other minority groups. Of the samples from Dire Teyara School, no respondent belongs to the Amhara and Harari ethnic groups. In the urban Model I school, where Oromo was the medium, 92.5 per cent were Oromo; 3.3 per cent were Amhara; and the rest were from minority ethnic groups. In the mainstream school, Yeshimebet, 64.7 per cent were Amhara; 11.8 per cent were Oromo; 10.9 per cent were Tigrawi; 5.9 per cent were Gurage; and 1.7 per cent were Harari. In the international school, 68.1 per cent were Amhara; 13.3 per cent were Harari; Harari and Oromo groups constituted 7.1 per cent each.

In order to further examine the ethnic background of the respondents, they were asked about the ethnic identity of their parents. On their father's side 43.7 per cent stated that they were Oromo; 21.1 per cent Amhara; and 16.1 per cent Harari. In addition to these three major ethnic groups, 3.8 per cent identified themselves as Gurage on their father's side; , 3.5 per cent were Tigrawi; 2.5 per cent Somali; and 2.1 per cent were foreign nationals . Other ethnic groups constituted 7.2 per cent of the respondents. On their mother's side, 44.7 per cent indicated they are Oromo; 22.6 per cent indicated they are Amhara; and 17.1 per cent Harari. The minority groups included Gurage 3.8 per cent; Tigrawi 2.5 per cent; Somali 2.2 per cent; foreign nationals 1.9 per cent; and other ethnic groups the remaining 5.2 per cent. In terms of ethnic distribution, there was thus no significant difference between the respondents' father and mother. In both cases, the major groups: the Oromo, the Amhara and the Harari constituted the majority.

First Language (Mother Tongue): In the samples taken, 40 per cent of the respondents stated that their first language was Oromo. The second largest group (30.5 per cent) said that Amharic was their first language, and the third largest group, the Harari speakers, constituted 22.1 per cent. The other minority groups made up the remaining 7.4 per cent: the Somali 1.2 per cent; the Gurage speakers 0.9 per cent; Tigrinya speakers 0.7 per cent; and other languages 4.6 per cent (Figure 5.2).

Interestingly, there was no necessary relationship between the first language of the respondents and their ethnic affiliation. That is, the distribution of first language did not always correspond to the ethnic distribution of the respondents. For instance, in Aw Abdal School, only 1.2 per cent identified themselves as Amhara but in the same school 8.4 per cent of the respondents stated that their first language was Amharic. In Gey Medresa 4.2 per cent identified themselves as Amhara while 12.5 per cent stated that their first language was Amharic. Conversely, in Aw Abdal 20.5 per cent of the respondents identified themselves as Oromo but only 15.7 per cent said that their first language was Oromo. Also, in Gey Medresa School 32.5 per cent identified themselves as Oromo, but only 15 per cent stated that their first language was Oromo. In the international SOS school 68.1 per cent identified themselves as Amhara, but 82.3 per cent said that their first language was Amharic. In the mainstream (Yeshimebet) school,

64.7 per cent identified themselves as Amhara, but 75.6 per cent of the respondents said that their first language was Amharic.

This fact suggests, against the widely held view, that there is no necessary association between ethnicity and language. At least in the Harari region, as these findings indicated, it is quite possible not to belong to the ethnic group represented by one's first language and to conceive of oneself as belonging to a different ethnic group whose language is not one's mother tongue.

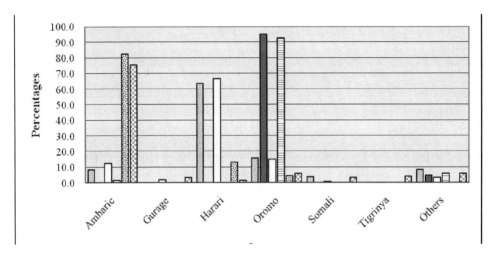

Figure 5.2. Distribution of First Language (Mother Tongue), by School

5.3.2. Parents

Sex and Age: The respondents totalled 222 parents of pupils in five different schools. Questionnaires from one school (Model I Elementary School) were not used in this study. Of the total parent respondents, 54.1 per cent were male and 45.9 per cent were female. In terms of age, about one-third of the respondents (32 per cent) were between the age of 40 and 49; 28.4 per cent were between 30 and 39 years of age. Younger parents (between 20 and 29 years) constituted 17.6 per cent and older parents (between the ages of 50 and 59) 10.8 per cent of the total population. Very few parents (4.1 per cent) were below the age of 20, and about the same percentage were over 60 years of age.

Level of Education: Out of the total respondents, a significant portion (24.3 per cent) was illiterate; 31.1 per cent had completed elementary education; 41.4 per cent were secondary school graduates. A few of the respondents (3.2 per cent) had some college education.

The level of illiteracy in rural areas is found much higher than it is in urban areas. Half (50 per cent) of the parent respondents residing in the rural area were illiterate; 38.9 per cent had elementary education; and only 11.1 per cent had secondary education. In urban areas the pattern was quite different. For instance, 69.8 per cent of the parent respondents in the mainstream school, Yeshimebet, had completed secondary education. Of these, around two per cent had college education. In Gey Medresa School, 32.6 per cent had completed secondary education, of which 4.3 per cent joined colleges. In Aw Abdal School, 46.5 per cent had completed secondary education and 9.3 per cent had a college education. In recent studies, Harari region has been described as having a highly educated and literate population (Gibb 2005, 1026) and the city of Harar is said to have the second-highest urban literacy rate in Ethiopia (Asante 2005, 1012).

Mother Tongue (First Language) vs. Ethnicity: Overall, 35.1 per cent of the respondents stated that their first language was Amharic, followed by Oromo 27.5 per cent and Harari 26.6 per cent. Other minority languages given as the first languages of the respondents included Somali 3.2 per cent and Tigrinya 2.3 per cent. Regarding ethnic identity, 33.3 per cent of the respondents were Oromo ethnic group; 26.6 per cent were Amhara; and 21.2 per cent Harari. Ethnically, the three major ethnic groups Oromo, Amhara and Harari constituted around 81 per cent of the respondents. Minorities included Somali (5.4 per cent) and Tigrawi (2.7 per cent) ethnic groups.

There was an interesting pattern regarding first language and ethnicity among the parent respondents. While 35.1 per cent stated that their first language was Amharic, only 26.6 per cent identified themselves as ethnically Amhara. On the other hand, 27.5 per cent of the respondents said that their first language was Oromo but 33.3 per cent of the respondents identified themselves as belonging to the Oromo ethnic group. Among the respondents 26.6 per cent stated that Harari was their first language; of these, 21.2 per cent identified themselves as Harari. There is a clear indication that Amharic has been acquired as a first language by numerous non-Amharas and that those who acquired Amharic as the first language are still maintaining their original ethnic identity, which is no longer represented by their first language.

5.3.3. Teachers

Sex and Age: A total of 87 teachers in the six schools completed the questionnaires. Of these, 58 per cent were male; 41.1 per cent were females; and the remaining 0.8 per cent didn't indicate their sex. Age wise, 34.4 per cent were between 20 and 29 years; 18.3 per cent were between 40 and 49 years of age; 16 per cent were between 30 and 39 years, while the remaining were either below 20 years of age or above 60.

Level of Training: Of the total respondents, 41.2 per cent had 12+1 level of training, i.e. one year of training after the completion of secondary education; 32.4 per cent had 12+2 level of training, i.e. two years of teacher training after the completion of secondary education; 8.8 per cent had only completed their secondary education. At least 73.6 per cent of the teachers had appropriate training for the level they were assigned to teach.

Mother Tongue (First Language) vs. Ethnicity: The distribution of mother tongue or first language of teacher respondents shows that the three major languages covered over 96 per cent of the sample population. Respondents that identified Amharic was their first language comprised 63 per cent; Oromo 22.2 per cent; and Harari 11.1 per cent. The remaining were minority language speakers. As regard to birth place, 43.2 per cent of the respondents were born in the Harari region; 50 per cent were born outside the region; and 6.8 per cent did not state their place of birth. In terms of ethnic composition, close to half of the respondents (45.6 per cent) identified themselves as belonging to the Amhara ethnic group. The second-largest ethnic group among teacher respondents was Oromo (26.6 per cent), followed by the Harari ethnic group (10.1 per cent).

This result suggests that among teachers, too, there was no one-to-one correspondence between first language and ethnicity. While 63 per cent of the respondents stated that Amharic is their first language but only 45 per cent identified themselves as Amhara. Conversely, while 22.2 per cent of the teacher respondents said that they spoke Oromo as a first language, 26 per cent of the respondents said they belonged to the Oromo ethnic group. Even though 11.1 per cent of the teacher respondents said that their first language is Harari, only 10.1 per cent of the respondents identified themselves as ethnic Harari. Once again, first language and ethnicity do not always reflect each other.

The overall characteristics of the respondents—pupils, parents and teachers—lead to the following generalizations.

- There are three major languages in the region—Amharic, Oromo and Harari—competing for dominance in the social and political life of the region.
- The association between ethnicity and first language is not always isomorphic. Contrary to the current official state policy, first language is not always the most important and prominent component in the constitution of ethnicity and self-identification in Harari region—nor is this necessarily the case elsewhere in Ethiopia. Ethnicity can be maintained without attaching importance to one's language. The simple equation that Language X necessarily represents Ethnic group Y is a faulty modus operandi, which does not reflect the sociolinguistic reality on the ground. Yet, this is the equation working in the political system of the day, and underlies the ideological foundations of the policy, such that language and ethnicity are taken as the main variables in constituting geo-political entities in the country.

5.4. Language Use

5.4.1. Pupils

The language use of the pupil respondents was investigated with reference to two domains: family and friendship. In both domains the three major languages: (1) Oromo, (2) Amharic, and (3) Harari were singled out, in that order. At home, 40 per cent of the respondents used Oromo; 33.8 per cent used Amharic; and 22.1 per cent used Harari. The remaining 2.1 per cent used other languages and 2.1 per cent did not state. Concerning language use with friends, the same pattern emerged, i.e. 36.4 per cent used Oromo; 34.8 per cent Amharic; and 24.6 per cent Harari. The remaining 1.9 per cent used other languages while 2.2 per cent did not state.

There is a correlation between language use and ethnicity; for example, the majority of the Amhara (92.1 per cent) said their first language was Amharic and 89.6 per cent of them said Amharic was the language they used with their friends. For 91 per cent of the Harari, their first language was Harari; for 75.4 per cent of them, Harari was the language they used with their friends; only 18 per cent of the Harari said they used Amharic with their friends. For 81.9 per cent of the Oromo, their first language was Oromo; 75.2 per cent of them reported that they used Oromo with their friends; 13.5 per cent used Harari with their friends; and 8.1 per cent reported using Amharic with their friends.

Among other minority groups, 54.9 per cent used Amharic as their home language, 17.1 per cent used Harari; and 14.6 per cent used Oromo. On the other hand, 13.4 per cent of the minority groups did not use the major languages at home. With their friends, however, 51.2 per cent of the respondents said they use Amharic; 34.1 per cent said they use Harari and 9.8 per cent use Oromo.

The language use situation, both at home and in social interactions, such as friendship indicates a high degree of language loyalty among the major groups. Among the minority groups, however, Amharic was the most widely used language both at home and with friends. More than half of the respondents stated that they used Amharic in those domains, an indication that Amharic has been maintained as a lingua franca. Interestingly, the second most widely used language among the minority groups, particularly with friends, was Harari (34.1 per cent). Even at home, Harari was used by a significant portion of the minority group respondents (17.1 per cent). Oromo is frequently used (14.6 per cent) at home among the minority groups, but less commonly used in social interactions.

5.4.2. Parents

Parents were asked about their language use in various domains, such as home, neighbourhood, in school environment with teachers of their children, with officials in government offices, and in social institutions.

At home, 41.1 per cent of the respondents stated that they used Amharic with members of their families while 27.9 per cent said they used Harari and 26.6 per cent used Oromo as their first language. With their neighbours, 45.5 per cent of the respondents used Amharic; 26.1 per cent used Harari; 24.8 per cent used Oromo; and 2.3 per cent of the respondents did not state the language they used with their neighbours.

In a school environment with teachers, 48.2 per cent of the parents used Amharic, 30 per cent used Harari and 16.7 per cent used Oromo. When talking to officials in the Harari region, 58.6 per cent of the respondents stated that they used Amharic, 18.9 per cent Oromo and 16.2 per cent used Harari. In social institutions, such as Idir (community associations for burial and mourning purposes) 46.4 per cent used Amharic, 25.2 per cent used Harari, and 20.3 per cent used Oromo.

In all the domains described in this chapter, Amharic was the most widely used language, followed by Oromo and Harari. Amharic was more commonly used for official purposes, such as in the school environment and in government offices. The language use pattern shows that all the three major competing languages were widely used in various domains within the region. The language use pattern further confirms that the status of the LWC, Amharic, has been well established; this is supported by the policy of the regional government, which has recognized Amharic as the official working language of the Harari Regional State.

5.5. Multilingualism in Harari

As has been discussed in the foregoing chapters, multilingualism in Harari Region, especially in the ancient city of Harar, is the norm rather than the exception. One factor that has contributed to the linguistic and cultural diversity of Harar is the fact that the city has been a centre of Islamic learning since the 16th century, and has attracted quite a large number of visitors of various ethnic groups. Waldron (1978, 239) recounts, "For at least four hundred years, the city [Harar] functioned as an important regional centre of Islam and a vital market area. Both influences served to connect Harar with internal Ethiopia, the Horn of Africa, and, indirectly, to the outside world". Another factor that facilitated multilingualism in Harar was assimilation of the neighbouring tribes through conversion to Islam. According to historical sources, the walled city of Harar, which housed predominantly a Harari-speaking community, had a wide range of interactions with the neighbouring Oromo and other Muslims in the area. Abir (1968, 9), for instance, notes, "The original population of Harar was of Hamitic stock called Adere. ... supplemented throughout the eighteenth and nineteenth centuries by Somali, [Oromo] and Afar settlers..."

Nevertheless, the city's linguistic landscape must have changed radically after the collapse of the last dynasty led by Amir Abdullahi and the subsequent incorporation of Harar into the Ethiopian empire (see Caulk 1971, 1977), which was followed by the introduction of Amharic by a large number of settlers from the highlands, mostly Christian immigrants. What is more, the assimilationist policies of successive regimes also contributed to the complex multilingual setting we have in Harar today. During the Haile Sellassie and Derg regimes, for instance, the Harari were forced to have primary education only in Amharic, like the rest of the country (see Chapter Three for details of the policies). Schools became a tool for the assimilation and integration of diverse languages and cultures. Socialization into being Ethiopian meant mastery of the Amharic language, which was a factor for upward mobility in the social and political hierarchy. The schools were considered as a melting pot to help create common social, political and economic ideals and hence were facilitators of multilingualism and multiculturalism. It is worthwhile noting that Harar was one of the first regional capitals where modern education was started at the turn of the 20th century.

A look at the demographic profile of the 1994 census shows that bilingualism correlates with urbanization while monolingualism is a feature of rural areas. The pattern of multilingualism (see Figure 5.3) shows that Oromo is the most widely spoken second language in the region, followed by Amharic and Harari. A similar pattern emerged in the sample population for this study (cf. Figure 5.4).

As already shown in the sample population, the three major linguistic groups in the Harari Region (Oromo, Amharic and Harari) together make up 92.6 per cent of the respondents, i.e. 40 per cent Oromo, 30.5 per cent Amharic and 22.1 per cent Harari, respectively.

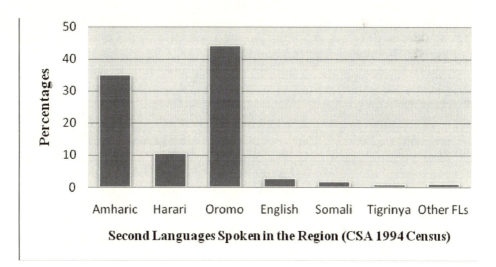

Figure 5.3. Patterns of Multilingualism in Harari Region

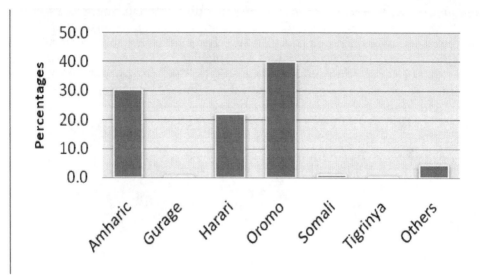

Figure 5.4. Distribution of Second Languages Spoken by Respondents

When asked whether they speak languages other than their mother tongue, 54.7 per cent of the total respondents (in the urban schools) claimed to be bilinguals in the various languages of the Harari region. The other 45.3 per cent stated that they did not speak other languages. Of those who claimed to be bilinguals, 53.1 per cent stated that they speak Amharic as a second language. This fact makes Amharic the first widely spoken second language in the urban areas. The second widely spoken language in the urban centre is Oromo with 18.9 per cent of the respondents. Harari seems to be the third widely spoken language (as a second language) in the city of Harar used by 8.9 per cent of the bilinguals.

As might be expected, in the rural areas the situation is different. The majority of the respondents in the rural school (92.7 per cent) claimed to be monolinguals, speaking no other language than their mother tongue, Oromo. Only nine respondents (7.3 per cent) stated that they did speak other languages. Of these, four spoke Amharic, and three claimed to speak English as a second language. The other two did not specify the language they speak. The high number of monolinguals in Oromo in the rural areas is not surprising given the sociolinguistic circumstances.

In the urban schools where Oromo is used as a medium of instruction, the pattern of multilingualism shows a different picture. In Model I Elementary School, 45 per cent said they speak also other languages; 90.7 per cent of these indicated they speak Amharic as a second language. A few (1.9 per cent) stated that they speak Somali. Ethnically, in Model I Elementary School the large majority (94 per cent) are Oromo. Bilingualism seems to be the norm in urban schools as opposed to the rural schools, where monolingualism dominates the scene. Urbanization clearly played a dominant role in influencing the pattern of multilingualism in the school since Amharic is the working language of the regional government and the lingua franca among the various ethnic groups residing in the city. It should be noted that although Oromo is the medium of instruction in Model I Elementary School, the language of administration is largely Amharic.

In terms of ethnicity, 47 per cent of the Amharas, 95.9 per cent of the Harari and 39.4 per cent of the Oromos said they were bilinguals[4]. Nearly all the Harari respondents, about half of the Amharas and over one-third of the Oromos were bilinguals. Of the total Amhara bilinguals, 28.6 per cent said they speak Oromo; 11.7 per cent said they speak Harari; 7.8 per cent said they speak Somali; 3.9 per cent said they speak Tigrinya; and 39 per cent said they speak English as a second language.

Among the Harari ethnic group, 63.2 per cent spoke Amharic as a second language while 19.7 per cent spoke Oromo as a second language. 5.1 per cent claimed to speak other foreign languages such as Arabic. Of the Oromo bilinguals 69.7 per cent spoke Amharic as a second language and 10.7 per cent spoke Harari as a second language. Other minority groups spoke Amharic (58.2 per cent), Oromo (10.9 per cent), Harari (9.1 per cent), English (5.5 per cent) and other foreign languages (7.3 per cent) as a second language.

Concerning the linguistic background of their families, 41.6 per cent of the respondents identified Oromo; 24.9 per cent Amharic; and 20.6 per cent Harari as their father's first language. Other minority languages spoken by the father were: Tigrinya (3.1 per cent), Gurage (1.6 per cent), and Somali (1.3 per cent). According to 24.8 per cent of the respondents, their mother's speak Amharic,; 20.2 per cent said they speak Harari; 18.1 per cent said they speak Oromo; 2.4 per cent said they speak Somali; 1.9 per cent said their mothers speak Tigrinya and 1.6 per cent said they are Gurage speakers. Speakers of various other Ethiopian languages jointly constituted 30.7 per cent. The pattern of first language is quite different between the two parents. On the mother's side the three competing major languages come in the order of Amharic, Harari and Oromo; while on the father's side the order changed to Oromo, Amharic, and Harari.

5.6. Language Attitudes

Blair (1990, 107–8) recognizes a three-fold distinction in the study of language use and language attitudes, namely *language use, language image* and *language posture*. Language use refers to what people are observed doing with the language whereas language image refers to what people

---

[4] Data on the distribution of second languages spoken by respondents are based on respondents' self-reports of the languages they know. These responses are often colored by contemporary attitudes about the various languages. How well speakers truly know the languages they say they know is not within the scope of this study. The purpose here is to identify the social characteristic which correlates with bilingualism and its distribution throughout the community.

think they do with the language. Language posture, on the other hand, has to do with what people claim they do with language or speech varieties they control, or think they control. According to the same author, in studying language attitudes a survey usually investigates only language posture since language image is rarely accessible to an outsider within the time span of the survey. Although it is important to investigate whether language image and language posture are similar or different within the region under study, the current research is limited to the study of language posture because the research method employed, i.e. the questionnaire method, is inadequate to elicit information about language image.

5.6.1. Pupils

First, we will consider pupil respondents' attitude towards choice of MOI, and the reasons they gave for the particular choice they made. The results obtained in this study show that 32.4 per cent of the respondents said they preferred Oromo as a MOI; 28.5 per cent chose English; 19.3 per cent Amharic; and 13.7 per cent Harari; only 2.2 per cent said their preference was Arabic and 3.3 per cent did not state their choice.

Generally, the respondents were positive towards the use of local languages as MOI. It is interesting to note, however, that they also showed a very positive attitude towards English and said that they would like English to be the MOI at the lower level (Table 5.1).

Table 5.1. Pupils' reasons for their choice of MOI

Reasons for choice	**Proportion of respondents (%)**
It is my mother tongue	47.79
It is suitable as a medium of instruction	25.27
It is an international language	22.53
It provides employment opportunities	17.50
It is a national/official language	11.87

Respondents' attitudes/opinions of the usefulness of MOI were assessed on a continuum from positive to negative with a neutral position in the middle. As to how they evaluate the language currently in use as a medium of instruction, the overwhelming majority, 80.8 per cent said it was "very useful"; 9.6 per cent said "useful"; and 5.8 per cent did not respond to the question. Only 1.3 per cent said they did not know. Among the reasons given, the main ones were pedagogic advantage, identity marking and language development.

Other follow-up questions were focused on the pedagogic advantages of the use of mother tongue in education. Respondents were asked whether the use of the mother tongue as a MOI has a facilitating function in the teaching-learning process and promotes the language and culture of the speakers; or whether it negatively affects the quality of education and limits mobility of freedom and economic opportunities.

The overwhelming majority, 91.7 per cent, of the respondents were positive; 4.9 per cent took a neutral position; while only a very small minority disagreed with the position that mother tongue education has a pedagogic advantage. Again, a large majority, 92.3 per cent, believe that the use of the mother tongue in education promotes the language and culture of the speakers. Only 5.3 per cent had a neutral position on this issue, while the rest disagreed. Conversely, 65 per cent of the respondents disagreed with the idea that the use of mother tongue negatively affects the quality of education; 28.2 per cent agreed with this opinion; 6.8 per cent of the respondents were neutral. About half of the respondents (50.5 per cent) thought that the use of mother tongue in education limits mobility of freedom and economic opportunities; 40.6 per cent disagreed with this view; nine per cent of the respondents could not decide on the issue.

In order to assess the attitude of the respondents on the use of the teaching of Amharic (the LWC and the official language of the nation) in the lower grades the pupils were asked to give their opinion along a continuum (strongly agree; agree; don't know; disagree, strongly disagree). About half of the respondents, 50.3 per cent, said they strongly agreed with the opinion that the teaching of Amharic is more important than the teaching of mother tongues; 13.4 per cent said they agreed with this opinion. On the other hand, 24.6 per cent said that they disagreed; 4.3 per cent strongly disagreed; 7.4 per cent were neutral.

Generally, there was a positive attitude among the respondents on the utility and pedagogic advantages of the mother tongue in education, and ultimately its promotion of cultural advancement. On the other hand, respondents were divided on the possible disadvantages of the use of the mother tongue in education, particularly whether the use of mother tongue limits mobility and economic opportunities. This means that although the overwhelming majority believed in the pedagogic advantages of the use of the mother tongue, they seemed to have doubts about its social and economic advantages. Quite a significant portion of the respondents also said that the use of the mother tongue may negatively affect the quality of education.

Problems Related to Mother Tongue Education—A general Account: One of the persistent problems in the use of vernaculars in primary education is the level of development of the languages and related issues of standardization. In order to assess the respondents' attitudes towards the capability of mother tongues for education, respondents were asked:

- whether there are conceptual or vocabulary problems in teaching science subjects in the mother tongue;
- whether there are translation problems or mistakes in the textbooks prepared in the mother tongue; and
- whether some subjects are more difficult to teach in the mother tongue.

From the responses given to these issues, it can be inferred that there are indeed problems related to the standardization of the languages being used in primary education, particularly problems related to vocabulary development and translation of textbooks into the mother tongues, as shown in Table 5.2.

Table 5.2. Pupils' responses on problems related to MTE

Problem	Responses (%)			x^2
	Yes	No	Don't know	
Conceptual errors	39.1	54.4	6.5	243.8*
Translation problems	44.5	45.6	9.9	167.9*

*The difference is statistically significant at 95 per cent confidence interval.

The problem of translating textbooks from Amharic into the vernaculars has been identified as a major problem in the country as a whole. Pursley (1997, 8), for instance, points out that in the southern region no attention has been given to translation techniques, especially during the initial years, because of an implicit assumption that if a person could speak both languages, she/he could translate between them. As a result, untrained persons have been involved in the translation of pupil texts and teacher guides. The same applies to Harari Region since no training was given in the techniques of translating textbooks from one language to another. This problem gives every sign of being a national problem observed in most regions launching mother tongue education.

The respondents particularly cited Mathematics and Environmental Science as subjects that were more difficult to follow in the mother tongue.

Another serious problem faced by multilingual education is the availability of resources and materials. To assess the respondents' attitudes towards the availability of resources and materials, they were asked:

- whether there are enough qualified teachers to teach in the mother tongue;
- whether there are enough reference books and magazines;
- whether there are enough reading materials; and
- whether there are enough materials for writing exercises.

Table 5.3. Attitudes of pupils concerning availability of enough qualified teachers and materials to MTE

Availability of resources and materials	Responses (%)			x^2
	Yes	No	Don't know	
Enough qualified teachers	88.9	11.1	—	158.7*
Enough reference books	68.0	19.5	12.5	371.4*
Enough reading materials	67.1	25.1	7.8	379.4*
Enough materials for writing exercises	66.4	24.2	9.4	355.2*
Mean average	72.6	13.7	7.4	528.4*

*The differences are statistically significant at 95 per cent confidence interval.

On average, a large majority of the respondents (72.6 per cent) said they believe that availability of resources and materials is fair and satisfactory (Table 5.3). The chi-square test, too, revealed a statistically significant difference between the groups.

The standardization of scripts is also an issue of serious concern among the users in particular and the public in general. An assessment was made on attitudes towards the appropriateness of the script currently in use and related problems. Half of the respondents stated that the script adopted to write the local vernacular properly represents the sounds of their respective languages; 24.6 per cent said that the script does not properly represent the sounds of their respective languages. Of the respondents, 25.4 per cent said that they did not know.

Given the youthful age and limited experience of the pupil respondents, it would be plausible to assume that they do not really have the knowledge and capacity to evaluate the scripts currently in use for mother tongues. The fact that a quarter of the respondents stated that they do not know whether the scripts properly represent the sounds of their language is an expected answer. Perhaps teachers or literate parents may have a better knowledge of the use of different scripts based on their own broader experience.

To look into their attitude towards the use of languages other than the MT in education, the respondents were asked to state their opinion on whether the teaching of other languages, such as Amharic and English exerts negative pressure on the teaching of mother tongues. The majority (73.3 per cent) of the respondents said that the teaching of other languages, such as the LWC and the international language does not exert pressure on the teaching of mother tongues; 22.4 per cent of the respondents expressed the opposite view stating that it does exert pressure on the teaching of mother tongues; 4.3 per cent took a neutral position. Generally, the majority of the respondents had a positive attitude towards the teaching of other languages in schools.

5.6.2. Parents

This section presents some of the attitudes and beliefs parents had about mother tongue education and related issues. Parents were asked to give their opinions on various issues, such as the choice of MOI, usefulness in teaching the MT, and the entry level they would prefer for English and the exit level they prefer for MT as medium of instruction.

Regarding their choice of MOI, respondents were asked which language of the region they would prefer to be used as a MOI to provide primary education to their children. Of them, 47.7 per cent stated that they would prefer Amharic, the LWC; 25.7 per cent said Harari; and 20.3 per cent preferred Oromo. A follow-up question was asked about the utility of teaching in the mother tongue and respondents were asked to give their opinion as to whether teaching in the MT is a good idea. The overwhelming majority, 96.4 per cent, said "yes". The reason why around half of the respondents nevertheless preferred Amharic to be the MOI for providing primary education–which seems to contradict the answer to the follow-up question–has to do with the aspirations of upward mobility for their children to enable them to compete at the national level.

Parents were also asked their opinion on which language they thought was more "useful" in the region. The three major languages, Amharic (32.0 per cent), Oromo (26.6 per cent) and Harari (22.1 per cent), were all considered useful languages in the region. Here again Amharic had a preferred position.

Following the educational policy instituted by the Ministry of Education in 1994, in all schools in the region the MT and English are introduced as of grade one. Respondents were asked about their opinion on the level they would like English to be introduced as a medium of instruction. A considerable majority, 59.6 per cent, preferred English to be introduced as a medium of instruction as of grade one, against the current practice; 15.7 per cent of the respondents said they would prefer English to be introduced as of grade seven, in line with the current practice; 7.8 per cent preferred it to be introduced as of grade five; and 3.0 per cent thought that introducing it as of grade six would be better.

Table 5.4. Preferred exit level for MT

Grade level	< 4	4	5	6	7	8	10	12	> 12	x^2
Respondents (%)	6.1	9.5	3.4	35.1	2.7	8.8	3.4	28.4	2.7	233.3*

*The differences are statistically significant at 95 per cent confidence interval.

Concerning the exit level of mother tongue as MOI currently in effect in the school system, 35 per cent of the respondents said that grade six should be the exit level for MT as a medium of instruction; 28.4 per cent preferred the exit level for MT to be 12th grade; 9.5 per cent said 4th grade; and 8.8 per cent preferred 8th grade to be the exit level for MT as MOI (Table 5.4). A minority of the respondents, 2.7 per cent, took the extreme position and stated that the MT should continue to be used even at tertiary level. Thus, although parents expressed a very positive attitude towards the use of Amharic (L2) and English (L3), they still considered the use of MT in schools useful.

5.6.3. Teachers

Teachers are the prime actors in any school and are the ones who are best informed about the concrete problems of mother tongue education. Having a better understanding of how teachers think about the mother tongue education within which they operate daily would thus give an important insider perspective. For this reason particular emphasis was given in the questionnaires to teachers opinions.

First, the attitude of teachers towards the use of MT in education was assessed. Respondents were asked to give their opinions about the utility of MT education, community involvement and preparations made before the implementation of the multilingual education policy, the impact the use of the MT may have on the quality of education, and the general attitude of teachers concerning MT education.

Regarding the advantages of using the mother tongue as a medium of instruction, 73.3 per cent of the respondents believed that it was very useful to learn in the MT; 19.8 per cent said it was useful. Only 3.5 per cent believed that it was not useful; another 3.5 per cent stated that they did not know. Those who said it is "very useful" and who said it is "useful" were asked to give reasons for their opinion. In response, 65 per cent of them said that because learning in the MT helps in the preservation of the culture of the community, including the language. Among the respondents, 18.8 per cent stressed its pedagogic advantage in easing the teaching-learning process; 11.3 per cent pointed out the economic advantage, i.e. it provides job opportunities within the region. A small proportion (2.5 per cent) of the respondents thought that using the MT in education has political significance. As revealed earlier, however, a solid majority stressed the issue of cultural preservation, which is related to linguistic rights and identity of the speakers.

The majority of the respondents said that they believe that using MT as a medium of instruction or teaching the MT as a subject at primary level would serve the purpose of preserving the identity of the speakers. Of the total respondents, 18.6 per cent took a neutral position; seven per cent disagreed with the opinion (Table 5.5).

About 36 per cent of the respondents said that they feel using the MT in primary education negatively affects the quality of education; 45.4 per cent disagreed with this view; a significant portion (18.6 per cent) could not give their opinion on the issue. Clearly opinion is divided. Concerning whether they think that the use of MT in education would limit intercultural communication and freedom of mobility, 40 per cent of the respondents said that they disagreed with this view. About one-third of the respondents agreed with the assertion that teaching and learning in MT limits intercultural communication and mobility. Again this is a division of opinion.

Table 5.5. Attitudes of teachers on the use of MT in education

Attitudes of teachers on the use of MT in education	Responses (%)					x^2
	Strongly agree	Agree	Can't decide	Don't agree	Totally disagree	
Help to preserve identity	61.6	12.8	18.6	3.5	3.5	100.19*
Negatively affects quality of education	26.7	9.3	18.6	32.6	12.8	15.99*
Limits intercultural communication	29.1	8.1	22.1	25.6	15.1	12.2*
Limits freedom of mobility	41.9	11.6	9.3	20.9	16.3	29.2*
Learning in L2 or L3 is more useful than learning in MT	37.2	16.3	15.1	15.1	16.3	16*

*The differences are statistically significant at 95 per cent confidence interval.

Concerning their attitude towards learning in languages other than the MT, such as Amharic (L2) and English (L3), 53.5 per cent of the respondents agreed that learning in the LWC or in an international language would be better than learning in the MT, whereas 31.4 per cent disagreed. This is an indication that a significant portion of teachers, who are the prime actors in the system, do not believe in the importance of teaching in the MT. It is possible that teachers may favour the teaching of the MT as a subject, yet for pragmatic reasons disfavour its use as MOI.

In a follow-up question, respondents were asked about teachers' initial reaction to the idea of teaching in the MT when the policy was first put into practice. The choices given were: 'most of them have accepted', 'half of them have accepted', 'less than half accepted', and 'it was rejected'. The majority, i.e. 60 per cent, of the respondents said most teachers immediately accepted the idea of using the MT as a MOI in education; 20 per cent thought that only half of the teachers were convinced of teaching in MT as a MOI; 8.1 per cent said that less than half of the teachers accepted the idea of teaching in MT, and seven per cent believed that teachers initially rejected the idea.

Ideally, in the formulation of a policy and its implementation strategies, the involvement of the community is highly desirable. Accordingly, respondents were asked whether there was any involvement of teachers, pupils and parents when the decision was made to use MT as MOI in education. The choices were: 'yes, there was a considerable discussion', 'there was fair level of discussion' and 'there was no discussion on the subject'. In response, 40.7 per cent of the respondents said that considerable discussion was held with the community; 24.4 per cent state that a fair level of discussion was held on the issue. Quite a significant portion of the respondents (22.1 per cent) asserted that no discussion made on the subject, and that the decision was made without proper consultation of the community.

Responding to whether schools had made any advance preparations to teach the MT as a subject as well as to use it as a medium of instruction, 54.7 per cent said that there was no preparation made at all; while 45.3 per cent stated that sufficient preparation was made. There was some variation in the responses given from one school to the next. Two-third of the respondents in the schools where Harari is used as a MOI stated that there was no preparation made to teach in the MT or to use the MT as a MOI. Of those who responded by saying that "no preparation was made", 51.1 per cent stated that teachers were not trained in the mother tongue, and 27.7 per cent said that there were not enough textbooks published/availed in the MT. About 19 per cent noted that the quality of teaching materials was poor.

Concerning whether parents had accepted the idea of teaching in the MT at the time of its implementation, 64 per cent of the respondents believed that most of the parents had accepted; while 20.9 per cent thought that only half of them had accepted the decision to use the MT.

Regarding the impact of teaching in MT on the quality of education and the performance of pupils, half of the respondents (50 per cent) said that they thought teaching in the MT did not make any difference in the quality of education. According to 12.8 per cent of the respondents, teaching in the MT raises the quality of education and the performance of pupils; 31.4 per cent believed that it lowers the quality of education. Those who said that it raises the quality of education gave a pedagogical reason: they said it facilitates the teaching-learning process because pupils are taught in the language they know and understand. About seven per cent of them said that they feel teaching in the MT increases the quality of education because it raises pupil's self-confidence and hence increases motivation for learning. On the other hand, those who believed that the use of the MT as a MOI decreases the quality of education reasoned out that the languages are not well developed for modern use, such as education.

Problems related to MTE (Teachers' perspective): The success or failure of any multilingual vernacular education depends greatly on the development of languages and availability of inputs to the curriculum. Respondents were asked a series of questions on problems persisting in the use of MT in general at both first and second cycle and teaching materials in particular, pupils' competence in the use of the MT and the availability of inputs in developing the languages being used in the school system. The data are summarized in Table 5.6.

Table 5.6. Teachers' responses to problems related to the use of MTE

Problems related to MTE	Responses (%)			x^2
	Yes	No	Don't know	
Inconsistency and lack of standardization in orthography	65.1	34.9	0.9	7.9
Variation in pronunciation	62.8	37.2	--------	5.6
Lack of proper terminology	65.1	34.9	--------	7.9
Proper representation of sounds by the script in use	52.3	23.3	24.4	13.9
Translation problems	36.0	37.2	26.8	1.7

*The differences are statistically significant at 95 per cent confidence interval.

As can be observed from Table 5.6, the majority of the respondents (about two-thirds) pointed out that in the teaching materials they saw inconsistencies in using the orthography, due to lack of standardization. They also said that they came across variations in the pronunciation of some words. Furthermore, they indicated that they encountered a lack of proper terminology for science subjects. On the use of scripts, over half the respondents said that they thought the sounds of their respective languages are well represented by the orthography, whereas about a quarter of the respondents said they believed the opposite. Another quarter of the respondents took a neutral position, perhaps due to a lack of technical knowledge about the nature of scripts and the techniques of designing orthographies. Thirty-six per cent of the respondents pointed out that the textbooks had translation problems as they were translated from Amharic textbooks; 37.2 per cent said they did not see any translation problems; and 26.8 per cent said they didn't know. On this issue, however, the difference was not statistically significant.

Teachers were also asked whether they had been forced to use any other (non-MT) language due to lack of proper terminology in the mother tongue. Thirty-six per cent of the respondents said that very often they used other languages, and 52.3 per cent stated that they occasionally used other languages while teaching in the MT due to lack of proper terminology. On the other hand, 11.6 per cent of the respondents stated that they never had this problem. Concerning how well the teaching materials were adapted to the cultural environment in which they are used, 57 per cent of the teacher respondents believed that the teaching materials well reflected the natural environment as well as the social, cultural and economic situation of the area. However, according to 26.7 per cent of the respondents, adaptation of textbooks to the cultural environment had been done in part, while 10.5 per cent stated that the teaching materials never reflect the environment in which they are being used.

Concerning whether they had come across any strange terminology or expression that is not common in normal speech, the majority of the teacher respondents (57 per cent) said that they had never come across such expressions, whereas 25.6 per cent stated that they did not know. However, 17.4 per cent of the respondents claimed that they had indeed come across such strange expressions and terminologies. On whether the teaching materials contained enough exercises on reading and writing skills, about two-thirds of the respondents said they thought that the teaching materials do contain enough of such exercises, while around one-third said they believed that there are insufficient exercises.

Concerning the pupils' competence in the language being used as medium of instruction, a large majority of respondents (70.9 per cent) said that they thought all pupils had proper competence in the language used as a medium of instruction; 20.9 per cent thought that most of the pupils did so.

Concerning whether they believed that the use of three languages (L1, L2, and L3) in as MOI in primary education has an impact on the competence of the pupils in these languages, 61.6 per cent of the respondents felt that such trilingualism helps in learning languages easily, whereas 24.4 per cent said that they believe it puts lots of pressure on pupils and makes the programme burdensome, and may also create confusion. As to 14 per cent of the respondents, the three-language model has both advantages and disadvantages.

The last issue looked into was the availability of inputs into MTE which may enhance the efficiency of the MT in the teaching-learning process. The questions raised were focused on the availability of dictionaries, supplementary materials, a teacher's guide, the methods of teaching L1 and L2, and whether the teaching materials really helped in developing the various skills in language learning. The responses are summarized in Table 5.7.

Around two-thirds of the respondents thought that there were enough dictionaries for use while about one-third stated that there were not enough dictionaries. Supplementary reading materials seem to be in scarcity if we consider the "No" responses (39.5 per cent) plus the 16.3 per cent of the respondents who said that they "do not know". In total these constituted 55.8 per cent of the respondents. Availability of a teacher's guide seems to be satisfactory—68.6 per cent said that teacher's guides are available.

On the teaching methods employed to teach L1 and L2, 64 per cent of the respondents stated that the approach was the same in the teaching of L1 and L2. However, 36 per cent of the respondents said there was a difference between teaching L1 and L2 and that quite different methods were employed

Table 5.7. Teachers' responses on the availability of inputs into MTE

Questions	Responses (%)			x^2
	Yes	No	Don't know	
Availability of dictionaries in the MT	64.0	36.0	—	6.7*
Availability of supplementary materials in the MT	44.2	39.5	16.3	7.7*
Availability of a teacher's guide	68.6	31.4	—	6.3*
Methods of teaching the MT similar to teaching other languages	64.0	36.0	—	6.7*
Content of teaching materials reflect the principle of learner-centeredness	60.5	39.5	—	3.8*
Teaching materials help to develop reading skills	70.9	18.6	10.5	55.4*
Teaching materials help to develop writing skills	64.0	20.9	15.1	36.8*
Teaching materials help to develop grammatical skills	65.1	16.3	18.6	39.1*

*The differences are statistically significant at 95 per cent confidence interval.

A majority (60.5 per cent) said that they believe the principle of learner-centeredness, i.e. the principle of reciprocal interaction in which pupils are active participants, was reflected in the teaching materials, while 39.5 per cent thought that the teaching materials did not reflect this principle. On the other hand, the majority of the respondents believed that the teaching materials are of help in developing the various language skills, such as reading, writing, and grammatical skills.

5.7. Summary

This chapter presented results of investigation of the language use situation, the attitudes and beliefs of pupils, parents and teachers about the use of MT in education as well as problems affecting MTE in the Harari region.

Results confirm that, unsurprisingly, the three major languages—Amharic, Oromo and Harari — are formidable competitors in the linguistic landscape of the region, and are widely used in various domains of the social and political life of the societies. All the three languages are in use in the school system; they are both taught as a subject and are used as media of instruction. The policy change in school reform brought the vernaculars, Oromo and Harari, into the forefront as identity-preserving languages. Amharic, despite the change of the policy that reduced its status significantly, is still the most widely used language, maintaining its status as a lingua franca used by various groups for inter-group communication. This is not surprising given the fact that Amharic is the official language of the regional and federal governments. It is also the language of wider communication across the country and the language of commercial activity; it has a well-developed literary language and teaching materials as compared to the vernaculars; it has trained human power particularly for elementary education. Among primary school teachers serving in the Harari region, as our sample shows, more than half are Amharic speakers who were most likely trained to teach in Amharic.

The observed patterns of multilingualism also confirm the fact that Amharic, Oromo and Harari are the three major languages of the region; as shown in this study, they are the most widely used second languages in the region. In urban centres, however, Amharic remains the dominant second language. Interestingly, nearly all the Harari respondents, around half of the Amharic speakers and over a quarter of Oromo respondents claim to be bilinguals. Factors that facilitated multilingualism and multiculturalism in Harari included urbanization and immigration of various groups, especially from the central highlands, assimilation of the various ethnic groups through conversion to Islam, and, more importantly, the change of language ideologies of the political systems over the last few centuries.

The attitudes of pupils, parents and teachers are generally positive towards MTE in general and the use of languages other than the MT in the school system in particular. Quite a large proportion of pupils (80.8 per cent), parents (96.4 per cent) and teachers (73.3 per cent) believed that using the MT as a MOI and teaching the MT as a subject are useful and further the purpose of preserving the cultural and linguistic heritage of the speakers, and also offer pedagogic advantages. All three groups, pupils, parents and teachers, are also positive about the use of languages other than the MT in the school system, although different respondents prefer different languages. For example, 28.5 per cent of the pupil respondents expressed their preference for English as a MOI. About half of the parent respondents stated that they would prefer Amharic to be the MOI in primary education. Teachers, on the other hand, seem to have both positive and negative attitudes. A significant portion of teacher respondents (53.5 per cent), though they do not seem to be against MTE, are of the opinion that learning L2 and L3 would be more useful than learning the MT.

Generally, however, all groups seem to agree with the three-language model of multilingual education advocated by UNESCO and supported by various educationalists. Studies show that this model is useful and practical because: (1) the pupils maintain their first language which has both pedagogic and cognitive advantages, and (2) the use of the first language in schools enhances the child's self-esteem and increases his or her motivation (Baker 1996, 208–209). The reason for the positive attitudes of pupils, parents and teachers towards L2, the LWC, and L3, the international language, is obvious and linked to the aspirations of upward mobility. Particularly the preference for English as a MOI at the lower level stems from a lack of awareness of the benefits of learning and teaching in the MT, and of the disadvantages of introducing English to children in a situation where English is neither the first language nor accessible to the majority. In particular, teachers must be aware of the system of education they are operating in. This is especially important given the gap already observed between the policy and its implementation model.

The results found in this chapter are also in line with the findings presented in the preceding and following chapters. Particularly in the area of language development and standardization of vernaculars used in the school system, there are persistent issues about which respondents recurrently expressed their opinions. Lack of preparation on the part of the schools before the implementation of the policy and inadequate involvement of the community in decision-making as well as in the implementation of the policy were concerns expressed by respondents. These facts have also been observed on the ground and are confirmed by interviews conducted with various stakeholders, such as teachers, school directors, policy-makers, parents, and the like. Among the problems related to the implementation model and mentioned by the respondents, the major impediments are: inconsistency in the use of orthography due to lack of standardization, variations in pronunciation of some words, and lack of proper terminology for certain subjects. The same problems were also identified through the study of the ethnography of schools (Chapter Four), the evaluation of orthographies (Chapter Six) and examination of the teaching materials (Chapter Seven) being used in the school system.

CHAPTER SIX
SCRIPT CHOICE: LINGUISTIC AND PEDAGOGICAL CONSIDERATIONS

6.1. Background

The choice of any script in writing an unwritten language is essentially a political decision and, by and large, falls within the jurisdiction of the power structure. All the same, adapting a particular script to a new language for the purpose of basic education brings into play a range of linguistic and pedagogical issues. The issues become more complex and intricate in sociolinguistic contexts where, by necessity, more than one script is involved in a multilingual education system.

As mentioned in the foregoing discussion, there are three writing systems in use in the Ethiopian education system: Ethiopic, Arabic and Latin. In most regions, there are at least three languages in use in primary education: the vernacular (L1), Amharic (L2), and English (L3). Amharic is the official working language of the nation and English is the international language. For these two languages, their scripts are already fixed: Amharic adopted the Ethiopic script and English uses the Latin alphabet. For the vernacular, the choice of script depends largely on the decision of the political structure and the ethnic composition of the particular region. In many regions in Ethiopia, the vernacular language very often serves as the only medium of instruction at the lower levels of primary education.

The trend in Harari region is, however, fundamentally different from other neighbouring regions, such as Oromia, for instance. The implementation model favours 'mother tongue education' rather than the monolithic use of a single regional language as a medium of instruction to be used by all children. As a result of this policy, various vernaculars have been officially recognized and introduced into the school system. This practice of recognizing different languages, both local and international, has led to the use of multiple scripts in primary education. Unlike most regions in Ethiopia, where the regional official language is the medium of instruction (although not necessarily the mother tongue of all the children), in Harari various languages are recognized side by side to serve as media of instruction, and the policy guarantees that parents will have options in choosing schools for their children. Thus, the implementation policy in Harari is unmatched elsewhere in Ethiopia as it allows the use of multiple languages and scripts within the region, even within the same school. Five languages have been recognized in Harari and used as media of instruction: (1) Amharic, (2) Oromo, (3) Harari, (4) English, and (5) Arabic. These five languages are each introduced into the school system with their own writing system. Three writing systems: (1) Ethiopic, (2) Arabic, and (3) Latin are used for the five languages. English, Amharic and Arabic already have established writing systems. Hence, it was only for the Oromo and Harari languages that new alphabets were adopted in the wake of the new educational language policy in 1991. Two languages, English and Oromo, use the Latin alphabet while two other languages, Amharic and Harari, use the Ethiopic script, albeit in different orthographic variations.

The purpose of this chapter is, therefore, to address a series of interrelated issues: What are the basic operational units of each writing system? On what level of linguistic structure are the units of a writing system interpreted? What are the possible kinds of positive and negative transfer that pupils might come across in acquiring reading and writing skills? Among languages that have adopted the same script, albeit in different orthographic variations, is there any kind of bridging mechanism put in place to maximize positive transfer in the teaching/learning process? In other words, how do we harmonize and bridge between the scripts in a particular school environment? Before dealing with these issues, let's first have a highlight of the nature of each script and the basic principles each writing system employs in encoding and decoding written messages.

6.2. The Ethiopic (*Ge'ez*) Writing System

The Ethiopic or Ge'ez writing system (the fidäl syllabary) was developed in Axum and its surroundings. Though some scholars disagree, the consensus is that the fidäl is derived from the South Arabian (Sabaean) writing system, which was transported across the Red Sea to Ethiopia (see Bender, Sydney, and Cowley 1976 for the details). It is important to clearly distinguish the origin of the Ethiopic script, the origin of the Ethiopic language family, and the origin of Ethiopian civilization—issues which are frequently (and wrongly) blurred and confused, as if they were a single issue. Regardless of the origin of the language and the civilization, the script is most likely to be derived from South Arabian, as can be learned by a brief glance at the South Arabian and Ethiopic letter-forms. South Arabian writing was a consonant-only alphabet; in Ethiopia this was transformed into a syllabary.

There is a general agreement among scholars of Ethiopian studies that the fidäl script was first designed and used for the classical language Ge'ez. Ge'ez has been serving as a literary and liturgical language of the Ethiopian Orthodox Church for many centuries. The Ge'ez script is highly systematic in its structural make-up, with consonant graphemes modified to represent the seven vowels, in which the vowels appear as diacritics added to the basic consonant symbol (Coulmas 1996, 17). Among the modern languages that adopted the Ethiopic writing system with some modifications are Harari and Amharic—languages now used as media of instruction in the Harari Region.

According to Daniels and Bright (1996) and Coulmas (1996), the main characteristics of the Ethiopic writing system (see Table 6.1) include the following:

(1) There are 26 main graphemes with seven vocalic subcategories for a total of 182 graphemes;

(2) It is an alpha-syllabic system: The basic graphemes that represent linguistic units are syllables but are based on alphabet; each "alphabetic" character has seven subcategories representing the vowels;

(3) The match between the script and the spoken language is not perfect but is quite good overall;

(4) The direction of writing is from left-to-right, another feature that distinguishes it from other Semitic scripts (except cuneiform);

(5) There are no differences in the way the graphemes are written at the beginning, middle or end of the word, unlike Arabic. Also, the graphemes have only one case—there are no capital or lower case graphemes in the system; and

(6) The basic system has no way of representing geminated consonants, and no way of distinguishing C and C↗.

Table 6.1. The Ethiopic script

Phonetic symbol	ä	u	i	a	e	↑	o
h	ሀ	ሁ	ሂ	ሃ	ሄ	ህ	ሆ
l	ለ	ሉ	ሊ	ላ	ሌ	ል	ሎ
⋏	ሐ	ሑ	ሒ	ሓ	ሔ	ሕ	ሖ
m	መ	ሙ	ሚ	ማ	ሜ	ም	ሞ
ś	ሠ	ሡ	ሢ	ሣ	ሤ	ሥ	ሦ
r	ረ	ሩ	ሪ	ራ	ሬ	ር	ሮ
s	ሰ	ሱ	ሲ	ሳ	ሴ	ስ	ሶ
q	ቀ	ቁ	ቂ	ቃ	ቄ	ቅ	ቆ
b	በ	ቡ	ቢ	ባ	ቤ	ብ	ቦ
t	ተ	ቱ	ቲ	ታ	ቴ	ት	ቶ
h▤	ኀ	ኁ	ኂ	ኃ	ኄ	ኅ	ኆ
n	ነ	ኑ	ኒ	ና	ኔ	ን	ኖ
◌	አ	ኡ	ኢ	ኣ	ኤ	እ	ኦ
k	ከ	ኩ	ኪ	ካ	ኬ	ክ	ኮ
w	ወ	ዉ	ዊ	ዋ	ዌ	ው	ዎ
◌	ዐ	ዑ	ዒ	ዓ	ዔ	ዕ	ዖ
z	☐	☐	☐	☐	☐	ዝ	ዞ
y	☐	ዩ	ዪ	ያ	ዬ	ይ	ዮ
d	☐	ዱ	ዲ	ዳ	ዴ	ድ	ዶ
g	ገ	ጉ	ጊ	ጋ	ጌ	ግ	ጎ
t'	ጠ	ጡ	ጢ	☐	ጤ	ጥ	ጦ
p'	ጰ	ጱ	ጲ	ጳ	ጴ	ጵ	ጶ
s'	ጸ	ጹ	ጺ	ጻ	ጼ	ጽ	ጾ
d◯	ፀ	ፁ	ፂ	ፃ	ፄ	ፅ	ፆ
f	☐	ፉ	ፊ	ፋ	ፌ	ፍ	ፎ
p	ፐ	☐	ፒ	☐	ፔ	☐	☐

6.3. The Arabic Writing System

In Harari region, as in other parts of Ethiopia, the variety of Arabic taught in the schools is classical Arabic. Spoken dialectal Arabic is alien to

Ethiopia. Arabic in Harari region is a language limited to basic literacy and religious studies; it is not used for day-to-day activities.

The Arabic writing system (see Table 6.2), an offshoot of the Aramaic-derived Nabataean script which originated in the fourth century CE in the Arabian Peninsula in the wake of the Islamic conquest, now serves over one hundred languages on three continents—Africa, Asia and Europe (Coulmas 1996). Although originally developed to write the Arabic language, the alphabet was adopted by many other languages around the world. In Ethiopia, at least informally, it has been adopted at various times under the label "ajami" (the use of Arabic letters to write a non-Arabic language) by various linguistic groups, such as the Oromo, Amhara, Harari, Somali and Argobba, and is still in use for writing religious manuscripts in Muslim-inhabited areas across the country.

Coulmas (1996, 18–22) notes that some basic principles of the Arabic writing system are the following:

1. Like most Semitic writing systems, Arabic orthography is basically a consonantal one;
2. It has 28 letters encoding consonants and long vowels and a number of optional diacritic lines for short vowels;
3. The letters are connected in writing. There are multiple forms of a single letter, depending on whether the letter is connected to the left, right, both, or neither;
4. Classical Arabic is a language that exists through writing. The written language is relatively far removed from the spoken dialects, allowing a range of different phonetic interpretations of the graphemes;
5. Distinct from the ancient Semitic alphabets, the Arabic alphabet is ordered according to graphic similarity of letters;
6. The direction of writing is from right-to-left as opposed to Ethiopic and Latin, which are written from left-to-right; and
7. Long vowels are represented by adding the corresponding semi-vowel letter; thus Ca: = C', Cu: = Cw, Ci; = Cy.

Table 6.2. The Arabic script

Name	Trans-literation[a]	Transcription	Numerical Value	Isolated	Final	Initial	Medial
'alif	' (a)	[ʔ]	1	ا	ا	–	–
bā'	b	[b]	2	ب	ب	بـ	ـبـ
tā'	t	[t]	400	ت	ت	تـ	ـتـ
ṯā'	ṯ, th	[θ]	500	ث	ث	ثـ	ـثـ
ǧīm	ǧ, dj	[dʒ]	3	ج	ج	جـ	ـجـ
ḥā'	ḥ	[ħ]	8	ح	ح	حـ	ـحـ
ḫā'	ḫ, kh	[x]	600	خ	خ	خـ	ـخـ
dāl	d	[d]	4	د	د	–	–
ḏāl	ḏ, dh	[ð]	700	ذ	ذ	–	–
rā'	r	[r]	200	ر	ر	–	–
zāy	z	[z]	7	ز	ز	–	–
sīn	s, sh	[s]	60	س	س	سـ	ـسـ
šīn	š	[ʃ]	300	ش	ش	شـ	ـشـ
ṣād	ṣ	[sˤ]	90	ص	ص	صـ	ـصـ
ḍād	ḍ	[dˤ]	800	ض	ض	ضـ	ـضـ
ṭā'	ṭ	[tˤ]	9	ط	ط	ط	ط
ẓā'	ẓ	[zˤ]	900	ظ	ظ	ظ	ظ
'ayn	'	[ʕ]	70	ع	ع	عـ	ـعـ
ġayn	ġ (ǵ), gh	[ɣ]	1000	غ	غ	غـ	ـغـ
fā'	f	[f]	80	ف	ف	فـ	ـفـ
qāf	q, ḳ	[q]	100	ق	ق	قـ	ـقـ
kāf	k	[k]	20	ك	ك	كـ	ـكـ
lām	l	[l]	30	ل	ل	لـ	ـلـ
mīm	m	[m]	40	م	م	مـ	ـمـ
nūn	n	[n]	50	ن	ن	نـ	ـنـ
hā'	h	[h]	5	ه	ه	هـ	ـهـ
wāw	w	[w]	6	و	و	–	–
yā'	y	[y]	10	ي	ي	يـ	ـيـ

SOURCE: Daniels and Bright (1996).

6.4. The Latin Alphabet

The Latin or Roman alphabet is perhaps the most widely used writing system in the world today. The Latin alphabet descended from the Etruscan alphabet, which was itself an offshoot of the Greek alphabet (Coulmas 1996, 285; Ober 1965). It is not clearly known how and when the Romans started to write but the earliest surviving specimen of writing in Latin has been dated about 600 B.C.; it must have been during the seventh century B.C. that the alphabet was introduced to the Romans by the Etruscans (Coulmas 1996, 285; Ober 1965, 133).

The Romans initially adopted 20 letters from the early Etruscan alphabet, but they kept on modifying the alphabet by leaving out some redundant symbols and adding new ones to suit their language. As a result, Latin became increasingly standardized. The direction of writing was also standardized as left-to-right around the 5th century B.C. (Coulmas 1996).

The Roman script has the following general features (Coulmas 1996; Ober 1965):

1) It is alphabetic in nature;

2) It is written from left-to-right;

3) It is un-phonemic in the sense that it is removed from a simple phonemic script which is often thought to be the hallmark of alphabetic notation; and

4) It has a great deal of irregularity (at least for English) and polyvalence (where the same letter represents several different sounds and vice versa) in its spelling system.

English has adopted the Roman alphabet with few additions (Ober 1965, 153) and the system makes use of at least three different units.

1) Individual letters and digraphs (e.g. ch, ou) and trigraphs (e.g. eau), which are interpreted as phonemes—distinctive sound units;

2) Letter sequences interpreted as morphemes—grammatical units; and

3) Orthographic words that cannot be reduced to grapheme—phoneme correspondences or morphological alterations.

Several attempts have been made to reform the English alphabet and orthography. Three particular cases stand out (Spolsky 2004, 34). One was an attempt made in the 19th and 20th century to simplify the spelling system and modify the shape of the letters. The other was a slightly more successful effort to develop a distinct and simplified spelling which was made in the US; many innovations were proposed by Noah Webster who published the American Dictionary of the English Language in 1828. A third attempt to simplify English spelling was made based on the principle of one letter for each sound in 1960's but failed to win popular support.

Although the Latin or Roman alphabet was originally developed for a single language, it has been adapted to a very large number of other languages over a wide geographical area. With minor variations, it is employed for writing modern languages, such as English, French, German, Polish, Turkish and many others (Ober 1965, 140). Today, within Ethiopia, numerous Cushitic and Omotic languages have adopted the Latin alphabet via English with minor modifications. These languages include: Oromo, Kambatta, Hadiyya, Sidama, Kefinoonoo, Shekinoonoo, Afar, Somali, Anuak, Jabelawi (Berta), Nuer, Majang, Konso, Gamo, Wolaytta, Gofa, Dorze, Gedeo (Burji) and Yem. Our interest in this chapter is to look at how Oromo has adopted the Latin alphabet via English and to investigate the various effects that cross-linguistic similarities and differences between the English and Oromo versions of the Latin Alphabet can produce in the teaching-learning process.

The following sections present discussion on how the LWC, Amharic, and the two vernaculars, Harari and Oromo, adopted their respective scripts; and examination of the impact of using multiple scripts with a single educational system and how it affects the teaching-learning process.

6.5. The Amharic Script

Amharic, which is the official working language of the Federal Government of Ethiopia with over 20 million speakers, has been officially written in an adaptation of the Ethiopic script since the 19th century, when it evolved into a full-fledged literary language replacing Ge'ez, under the language policy of Emperor Tewodros (Bahiru 2002) (see Chapter Three). Amharic is one of the media of instruction in the ancient city of Harar in at least five mainstream schools. It is worthwhile examining how Amharic has adapted and modified the Ge'ez script, and the ideological skirmishes it has passed through in the process.

Amharic has adopted the entire syllabary of Ge'ez (fidäl) without any modifications. As a result, it retained from Ge'ez extra graphemes that were unnecessary in Amharic (Bender, Sydney, and Cowley 1976, 125). This problem of over-differentiation (having more than one symbol for a single sound) has, therefore, been a typical characteristic of the Amharic script. One further deficiency of the fidäl mentioned by Bender, Sydney, and Cowley (1976, 125) is lack of marking of gemination of consonants. Amharic, like Ge'ez, has a productive process of consonant gemination that has both lexical and grammatical functions. The issue of consonant gemination and vowel length vis-a-viz the Ethiopic script aroused a heated public debate in the early 1990's. The idea that the Ethiopic fidäl is inherently incapable of marking such features, which are widespread in Cushitic and Omotic languages, is a misconception that came to the fore during the implementation of the educational language policy of Ethiopia in the last fifteen years or so. Suitably modified, it is capable of marking both features as demonstrated in the orthographies of the Cushitic languages K'abena (Moges 2005) and Xamtanga (Gebre 2004).

Language Ideologies and Challenges of Multilingual Education...   109

Amharic has added new graphemes to the system in order to accommodate consonants that do not exist in Ge'ez, yielding 33 basic graphemes in total (see Tables 6.3 & 6.5). Like Ge'ez the writing system of Amharic is alpha-syllabic in that it represents the consonants by independent basic graphemes and the vowels by way of diacritics attached to these basic graphemes. The direction of writing and the alphabetical order of the graphemes are the same as in Ge'ez.

Table 6.3. The Amharic script (Fidäl)

Phonetic symbol	ä	u	i	a	e	↑	o
h	ሀ	ሁ	ሂ	ሃ	ሄ	ህ	ሆ
l	ለ	ሉ	ሊ	ላ	ሌ	ል	ሎ
▲	ሐ	ሑ	ሒ	ሓ	ሔ	ሕ	ሖ
m	መ	ሙ	ሚ	ማ	ሜ	ም	ሞ
ś	ሠ	ሡ	ሢ	ሣ	ሤ	ሥ	ሦ
r	ረ	ሩ	ሪ	ራ	ሬ	ር	ሮ
s	ሰ	ሱ	ሲ	ሳ	ሴ	ስ	ሶ
●	ሸ	ሹ	ሺ	ሻ	ሼ	ሽ	ሾ
▢●= k']	ቀ	ቁ	ቂ	ቃ	ቄ	ቅ	ቆ
b	በ	ቡ	ቢ	ባ	ቤ	ብ	ቦ
t	ተ	ቱ	ቲ	ታ	ቴ	ት	ቶ
♦●	ቸ	ቹ	ቼ	ቻ	□	ች	ቾ
h▤	ኀ	ኁ	ኂ	ኃ	ኄ	ኅ	ኆ
n	ነ	ኑ	ኒ	ና	ኔ	ን	ኖ
✱	ኘ	ኙ	ኚ	ኛ	ኜ	ኝ	ኞ
✎	አ	ኡ	ኢ	ኣ	ኤ	እ	ኦ
k	ከ	ኩ	ኪ	ካ	ኬ	ክ	ኮ
x	ኸ	ኹ	ኺ	ኻ	ኼ	□	ኾ
w	ወ	ዉ	ዊ	ዋ	ዌ	ው	ዎ
✍	ዐ	ዑ	ዒ	ዓ	ዔ	ዕ	ዖ
z	□	□	□	□	□	ዝ	ዞ
☾	ዠ	ዡ	ዢ	□	ዤ	ዥ	ዦ
y	□	ዩ	ዪ	ያ	ዬ	ይ	ዮ
d	□	ዱ	ዲ	ዳ	ዴ	ድ	ዶ
⚕☾	ጀ	ጁ	ጂ	ጃ	ጄ	ጅ	ጆ
g	ገ	ጉ	ጊ	ጋ	ጌ	ግ	ጎ
♦●	ጠ	ጡ	ጢ	□	ጤ	ጥ	ጦ
♦●●	ጨ	ጩ	ጪ	ጫ	□	ጭ	ጮ
▢●	ጸ	ጹ	ጺ	ጻ	ጼ	ጽ	ጾ
s'	ፀ	ፁ	ፂ	ፃ	ፄ	ፅ	ፆ
d○	ፈ	ፉ	ፊ	ፋ	ፌ	ፍ	ፎ
f	□	ፉ	ፊ	ፋ	ፌ	ፍ	ፎ
p	ፐ	□	ፒ	□	ፔ	□	□

As aforementioned, the Amharic orthography adopted from Ethiopic has some problems of over-differentiation. It has five superfluous graphemes (each with 7 variants as usual) (see Table 6.4).

Table 6.4. Over-differentiated graphemes in Amharic

Phonetic symbol	ä	◆	ℋ	☺	ℳ	↑	□
ʌ	ሐ	ሑ	ሒ	ሓ	ሔ	ሕ	ሖ
ś	ሠ	ሡ	ሢ	ሣ	ሤ	ሥ	ሦ
h▣	ኀ	ኁ	ኂ	ኃ	ኄ	ኅ	ኆ
⌀	አ	ኡ	ኢ	ኣ	ኤ	እ	ኦ
dO	ዐ	ዑ	ዒ	ዓ	ዔ	ዕ	ዖ

Orthographic reform for Amharic has been an issue of serious debate among academics, politicians, church scholars and the clergy for more than half a century. Several proposals have been forwarded but none has ever been realized or put into action due to the political and ideological sensitivity of the issue. As can be gathered from the many papers and suggestions (Academy of Ethiopian Languages 1973 (E.C.)) made on the subject of orthographic improvement, those who object to a revision of the fidäl hold that it should be preserved untouched as part of the cultural heritage of the people. Those who have supported a revision represent several lines of argument. These can be grouped roughly into three approaches:

a) Those who have proposed a radical change, suggest that the Latin alphabet should be adopted alongside the Ethiopic for teaching in the schools, and in general for most modern fields of application. The reason they gave was that it would facilitate technological advancement, and they cited Turkey as an example. The Turkish case is particularly interesting as there was a shift in language ideology that led to the change of script. During the 9th and 10th centuries, when the Turks were Islamized, Arabic script was adopted; a millennium later, when Turkey became a republic in 1923, in order to 'modernize' and 'westernize' Turkish society, Latin script officially replaced the Arabic script (Salzmann 1998, 286). The opponents of this view refer to Japan as an example where an indigenous syllabic writing system has been maintained and developed for modern use.

b) Those who proposed major modification, i.e. separating the vowels and consonants in writing as in the alphabetic systems.

c) Those who proposed minor modifications, i.e. eliminating the redundant or the extra graphemes used to represent the same sound— in other words, avoiding over-differentiation in the orthography. The suggestion has been to follow the principle of 'one letter for one sound'.

Language Ideologies and Challenges of Multilingual Education...   111

The first proposal, dating back to the time of Haile Sellasie, has never had much support. Under the Derg, the Academy of Ethiopian Languages (now the Ethiopian Languages Research Centre, ELRC) supported the third position of making minor modifications. According to their proposed revision, the extra symbols ሐ ሠ ኀ ዐ and አ not ዐ (recall Table 6.4) were to be eliminated, and some modifications were to be introduced to give uniformity in the representation of vowels. However, since the Academy had (and has) no legal power to put its decisions into practice, the proposal ended up as a mere research paper. The ELRC, nevertheless, persisted in its decision and used its revised version of the Amharic script in a recently published Amharic Dictionary in 2000. This practice has neither been followed by any other institution nor approved by concerned authorities, mainly in order to avoid a possible clash with the Ethiopian Orthodox Church and other sectors of the public. The Academy's power was merely theoretical, and in a script reform much depends on the ideology of the power structure and the society at large (cf. 2.1. on language ideologies).

As a comparison of Table 6.1 (Ethiopic script) and Table 6.3 (Amharic script) shows, Amharic has added seven basic graphemes (Table 6.5) for those sounds mostly palatals that are lacking in Ge'ez but present in Amharic.

Table 6.5. New graphemes developed for Amharic

Phonetic symbol	ä	◆	ℋ	♋	ℳ	↑	□
ʃ	ሽ	ሹ	ሺ	ሻ	ሼ	ሽ	ሾ
tʃ	ች	ቹ	ቺ	ቻ	☐	ች	ቾ
ɡʲ	ኝ	ኙ	ኚ	☐	ኜ	ኝ	ኞ
ʔɡʲ	ዥ	ዡ	ዢ	ዣ	ዤ	ዥ	ዦ
t◆	ጭ	ጩ	ጪ	ጫ	☐	ጭ	ጮ
✱	ኝ	ኙ	ኚ	ኛ	ኜ	ኝ	ኞ
☒	ኽ	ኹ	ኺ	ኻ	ኼ	☐	ኾ

The new graphemes were systematically designed from the existing symbols by adding regular diacritic marks. The palatal signs were derived from the signs for the corresponding alveolars, generally by adding a bar at the top of the grapheme; similarly, the velar fricative [☒ ✺ was represented with a sign derived from the sign for the velar stop [&✺. The ordering of the Amharic graphemes is simply taken over from that of Ge'ez; the newly added graphemes were ordered directly after the grapheme from which they were derived.

6.6. The Harari Script

The tradition of writing in the Harari language goes back to the 16th century when Harar was a major city of Islamic learning in the Horn of Africa. The city of Harar is considered one of the first places in Muslem Sub-Saharan Africa to have employed the Arabic script to write the local language. According to Banti (2005), the first dated manuscripts of Harari texts written in *ajami* (Arabic script) are from the end of the 17th century and are mainly religious texts (see Figure 6.1).

Figure 6.1. The Oldest Known Writing in Harari Using the Arabic Script (Dated End of 17th Century)

SOURCE: Banti (2005)

With the incorporation of Harar into the Ethiopian state towards the end of the 19th century, Amharic was increasingly used in the city. Some people tried to write the Harari language using the Ethiopic script, the best-known example being the *Gey aja'ib-zo* by Takle Haymanot, which was published by Conti Rossini in 1919 (Banti 2005) (see Figure 6.2).

Language Ideologies and Challenges of Multilingual Education... 113

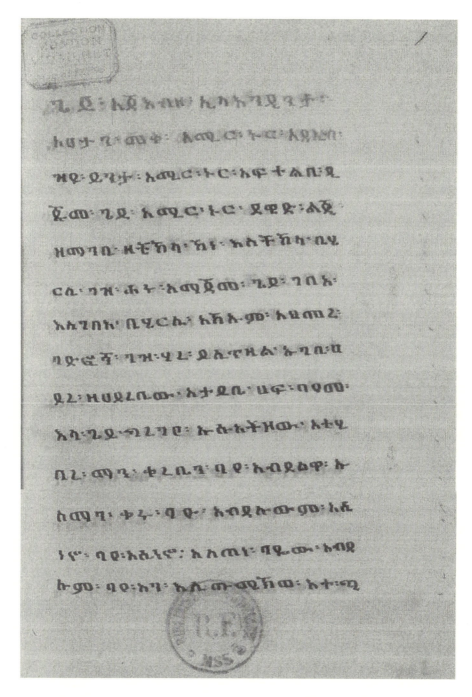

Figure 6.2. The First Known Writing in Harari Using the Ethiopic Script, Known As *Gey aja'ib-zo* by Takle Haymanot, Published by Conti Rossini in 1919.

SOURCE: Banti (2005)

Since then, the Ethiopic script has been in wide use for over 40 years due to the literacy campaign launched by Ephraim Isaac.* Historical sources indicate that the Ethiopic script had also been used earlier by Lij Eyasu, in the underground coded letters he exchanged with his supporters in Harar, which was regarded as his stronghold (Kinfe-Regb 1982). As recently as 1991, in the wake of the political and ideological changes that occurred after the fall of the military regime, there was a movement to use the Latin alphabet but this failed after a year or so due to the resistance of the public. The Ethiopic script then took over and is still officially in use.

Writing in Harari has, therefore, passed through several stages employing various scripts—Arabic, Ethiopic and Latin. Although the Ethiopic script has now been adopted for official purposes, the writing of Harari using Arabic script (*ajami*) is very much alive today, and old hymns and prayers written in Arabic script are devoutly copied and read or sung during the religious gatherings such as the *zikri's*. New hymns and hagiographies of the major saints of Harar are still being composed today, some of which have been printed in Arabic script in recent years (Banti 2005).

Harari is an Ethio-Semitic language like Amharic and Ge'ez. Phonologically, however, it is slightly different from Amharic. One difference relates to its vowel system. Harari has distinctive vowel length, whereas in Amharic and Ge'ez this feature is absent. In the consonantal system, there are two pharyngeal sounds (⊥ and ⊿) which do not exist in Amharic. Furthermore, whereas Amharic has adopted the Ge'ez script without any modification, Harari has left out the extra symbols and adopted only those relevant to the system of the Harari language, thereby removing the problem of over-differentiation. As a result, Amharic has 33 graphemes while Harari has only 23 graphemes (Table 6.6).

---

* Ephraim Isaac was one of the pioneering figures in campaigning for and launching the literacy programme for adults in the early 1950s.

Table 6.6. The Harari script, which is currently in use

Phonetic symbol	ä	u	i	a	e	ɨ	o
∧	ሐ	ሑ	ሒ	ሓ	ሔ	ሕ	ሖ
●	ለ	ሉ	ሊ	ላ	ሌ	ል	ሎ
○	መ	ሙ	ሚ	ማ	ሜ	ም	ሞ
□	ረ	ሩ	ሪ	ራ	ሬ	ር	ሮ
♦	ሰ	ሱ	ሲ	ሳ	ሴ	ስ	ሶ
◆	ሸ	ሹ	ሺ	ሻ	ሼ	ሽ	ሾ
□ [=k']	ቀ	ቁ	ቂ	ቃ	ቄ	ቅ	ቆ
∂	በ	ቡ	ቢ	ባ	ቤ	ብ	ቦ
♦	ተ	ቱ	ቲ	ታ	ቴ	ት	ቶ
♦♦	ቸ	ቹ	ቺ	ቻ	□	ች	ቾ
■	ነ	ኑ	ኒ	ና	ኔ	ን	ኖ
✳	ኘ	ኙ	ኚ	ኛ	ኜ	ኝ	ኞ
⌇	አ	ኡ	ኢ	ኣ	ኤ	እ	ኦ
&	ከ	ኩ	ኪ	ካ	ኬ	ክ	ኮ
⊠	ኸ	ኹ	ኺ	ኻ	ኼ	□	ኾ
♦	ወ	ዉ	ዊ	ዋ	ዌ	ው	ዎ
⌘	□	□	□	□	□	ዝ	ዞ
⊠	□	ዩ	ዪ	ያ	ዬ	ይ	ዮ
♎	□	ዱ	ዲ	ዳ	ዴ	ድ	ዶ
♎℃	ጀ	ጁ	ጂ	ጃ	ጄ	ጅ	ጆ
℣	ገ	ጉ	ጊ	ጋ	ጌ	ግ	ጎ
♦	ጠ	ጡ	ጢ	□	ጤ	ጥ	ጦ
➶	□	ፉ	ፊ	ፋ	ፌ	ፍ	ፎ

6.7. The Oromo (Qubee) Orthography

Hayward and Mohammed (1981) in their article *The Oromo Orthography of Bakri Sapalo'* trace one of the earlier Oromo writings in the Arabic script. According to them, Bakri, who lived in Hararge, wrote poems in Oromo using Arab script. In 1956 he invented an indigenous Arabic-based Oromo orthography (ajami) in the then Obora *Awraja*[5] of Hararge region. He taught this orthography to his pupils and other people in the area, and wrote poems and letters using it. Also other people started using this alphabet. However, the government opposed the spread of the orthography and put Bakri into confinement in Dire Dawa (Hayward and Mohammed 1981).

Andrzejewski (1977) in his article, *Observation of the Present Oromo Orthography"* mentions the contribution of Onesimos Nesib, an Oromo who lived in Sweden, and Aster Ganno. According to him, these two Oromo individuals published religious and secular texts in Oromo in 1894

---

[5] Awraja was an administrative structure between district (there were many districts within an awraja) and province (there were many awrajas within a province).

using the Ethiopic script (fidäl), adapting the script by adding a diacritic to represent the implosive consonant /ɗ/. Sometime later in 1898 Onesimos Nesib with the help of Aster Ganno, translated the Holy Bible into Oromo using the Ethiopic script. Onesimos, according to Teshome (1979, 25), was one of the few Ethiopians educated by the Swedish Evangelical Mission in the 19th century; he later became very active in the work of the mission in Ethiopia and took part in the translation of the Holy Bible into Oromo.

Andrzejewski (1977) further notes that after the 1974 revolution, *Barisa,* the first Oromo newspaper, appeared in Ethiopic script as a weekly publication. *Barisa* focuses on different issues: news, poems, etc. According to Andrzejewiski (1977), people in Bale and Harar areas have used Arabic script to write Oromo with some modifications; most of the texts are religious poems like the *manzuma (zikri).*

Latin script was used before the 1974 revolution for writing Oromo by some members of the Oromo Diaspora in Europe (Andrzejewski 1977). Texts written in Latin script were smuggled into the country before the revolution as well. One such example is the book entitled *Hirmaata Dubbii Afaan Oromo,* meaning 'Oromo parts of speech', which was written in France in 1973. The book used the Latin script with some modifications, employing superscripts and diacritics.

The orthography currently in use, known as Qubee (see Table 6.7 for the consonants), was developed in 1991 based on the Latin alphabet.

Table 6.7. Graphemes representing Oromo consonants as given in the official teaching materials for primary education

Oromo Orthography							IPA Equivalents						
b	c	d	f	g	h	j							
k	l	m	n	p	q	r							
s	t	v	w	x	y	z							
ch	dh	ny	ph	sh	ts	zy							

The vowels are represented using the canonical IPA values of the normal vowel letters; long vowels are represented by writing the vowel twice, like aa and ee.

Askale (1998) points out that the design of the Oromo orthography lacked any proper planning stage due to the rush that followed the overthrow of the Derg regime. At the time, there was no organized body that could sit down and work out an effective implementation strategy as to how the orthography should be designed and put in place for official use. Hence, interested groups designed the orthography as they wished and started to teach it. Because of this, according to Askale (1998), the orthography has the following shortcomings:

- While some foreign phonemes are present in the orthography as if they were native phonemes of the language (e.g. graphemes such as **ts, p, v**, and **zy**), some native phonemes, such as the /◌/ are not represented;

- Inconsistencies can be observed in different books authored by different people in using the alphabet. Different books show a different number of graphemes. Although the phonemic inventory of Oromo shows 24 consonants and 5 vowels (long and short), the number of graphemes used in six different books published in Oromo varies from 29 to 33;

- There is also confusion in denoting word boundaries and in combining morphemes into words. Word boundaries seem to be random and inserted at the whim of each writer. Dyken and Kutsch Lojenga (1993, 18) quoted in Askale (1998, 329), state, "Mismatches between spoken and written words can confuse a beginner in his efforts to read and write. They can also hinder the quick recognition of words, essential for fluent reading"; and

- Adding to these confusions is an inconsistency in the alphabetical order of graphemes, which varies from one language-pedagogical book to the other.

Askale concludes that the whole undertaking is a promising beginning but needs to go through the process of evaluation and re-evaluation of the orthography.

6.8. Harmonization of Orthographies: A Way Forward

Spolsky (2004, 29) discerns two conflicting criteria by which the efficacy of writing systems can be judged: (1) the technical/psycholinguistic, and (2) the sociolinguistic/attitudinal aspects. The former includes issues, such as ease of learning, ease of reading and writing as well as transferability to other languages; the latter has to do with ideological, political or religious factors.

From the technical and psycholinguistic perspectives, designing orthography or adopting an existing orthography presupposes a good and accurate description of the phonology of the language and familiarity with its sound pattern. Moreover, in the process of designing a new orthography, any existing orthographies already in use in the area or in the school system should be taken into consideration, especially when two or more languages adopt the same script. These two conditions are essential in designing a pedagogically and linguistically sound practical orthography. In a situation where multiple scripts are in use, harmonization of the different orthographies would help in facilitating the teaching-learning process.

Technically, there are two types of scripts in use in the region: alphabetic and syllabic. The alphabetic script is a writing system where pupils must recognize the correspondence between letters (graphemes) and phonemes (distinctive sound units). The syllabic is a system in which pupils must recognize the correspondence between symbols and syllables. Harari and Amharic follow the syllabic system (fidäl) while English and Oromo use the alphabetic writing system; Arabic uses a consonant-only alphabet. Pupils are thus expected to master different orthographies that employ different principles. As Odlin (1989, 124) notes, developing the skills of writing and reading involves not only a mastery of individual symbols but also of systems of symbols. It should also be noted that similarities and differences in writing systems can result in both positive and negative transfer (ibid, 127). From a technical point of view, the characteristics of a good practical orthography should include accuracy, i.e. the representation of all distinctive sounds in the language, consistency and transferability from one language to the next.

In an ideal situation, the orthography should provide an adequate representation not only of the sounds of L1 (clearly the first priority) but also of sounds borrowed from other languages, such as L2 or L3. An ideal writing system should also include both segmental and suprasegmental (tonal) features of the language under consideration. Whether the nature of the orthography should be phonemic or not has been an issue of contention amongst linguists. Some linguists argue that each phoneme should be consistently represented by the same symbol, the idea of 'a constant visual image'; in the minds of the speakers it is only one phoneme, hence it should have one symbol. Gudschinsky (1957) writes, "The practical orthography should in general symbolize the underlying form of the phonemes rather than the phonetic form that is actually pronounced". Those who hold this view emphasize that phonemic representation would enhance ease of learning, i.e., in a strictly phonemic system, a pupil can pronounce every word in his/her language as soon as he/she knows the pronunciation of each letter. On the other hand, distinct representation of some of the different allophones could be useful if another language involved in the school system uses the same writing system—as in the case of English in Ethiopia, which may have separate phonemes and symbols for what are allophones in the L1, Oromo. For instance, the velar nasal /ŋ/ is a phoneme in English but an allophone in Oromo, and as such requires a distinct graphic representation (ng) when writing English but not Oromo.

Having the same writing system, i.e. alphabetic for Oromo and English or alpha-syllabic for Harari and Amharic, can be a tremendous advantage for learners if bridging between the two varieties of the same writing system is seriously taken into consideration. The most basic difference between the Oromo and English orthographies is that the Oromo orthography is close to phonemic, whereas the English orthography is highly un-phonemic; this makes the transfer of skills very complicated and also causes serious spelling problems in the case of English. The problem becomes more serious when we compare the Oromo (Qubee) orthography with that of English: some symbols such as [ph, ch, x, q'] represent different sounds in Oromo [ph, ch, x, q'] and in English. Note that the entry level at which both languages, and hence both orthographies, are introduced is the same, grade one. Young pupils are thus confronted with this confusion of symbols and spelling from the very beginning.

On the other hand, the [h] grapheme is used to represent the voiceless glottal fricative phoneme /h/, which is an independent phoneme in the language; but it is also used as a diacritic to represent various features. For example, in the graphemes [ch] and [sh] the [h] represents place of articulation (palatal), and in [ph] and [q'] it stands for the feature ejective. Hence, the [h] symbol is used inconsistently representing various features. The grapheme [y] is likewise used to represent the palatal phoneme /y/ but also serves a diacritic mark as in [ny] to indicate the palatal feature. This problem of inconsistency is similar in many Cushitic languages (see Yri 2004) for Sidamo, for instance). Inconsistency, in turn, affects transferability from one language to the other.

It would be possible to prepare the orthographies and teaching materials specifically to help pupils in bridging to the second language, i.e. the materials could be designed so as to make it easier for pupils to transfer their reading skills more effectively from Oromo to English or from Harari to Amharic. For instance, bridging between the teaching materials could help in avoiding the confusion in teaching the letter 'x', which represents the phoneme /t'/ in Oromo but /ks/ in English or the letter 'q', which represents the Oromo phoneme /k'/, etc. In bridging between the materials of two languages used in the same school, the material should first introduce those letters that have the same sounds in both languages. Words and sentences that use these letters or sounds should be taught and drilled first so that pupils will have the opportunity to use their reading skills in the other language immediately. Focusing on the similarities of the two writing systems could give learners a head start in reading and writing both Oromo and English. Only then should any new letters, i.e. letters that are used in English but not in Oromo, be taught. Where letters have different sounds in the two languages, they will have to be carefully taught to show their correct pronunciation in each of the two languages. This would give pupils the opportunity to make interlingual identification of familiar letters and thus begin their mastery of both orthographies on the basis of their similarities (Odlin 1989, 125). This approach would help considerably in reducing the time needed to get literate in both Oromo and English. Unfortunately, because this has not been done, neither for Oromo nor for any other language taught in the Ethiopian schools, textbooks must devote much space to explaining the differences and similarities of the two writing systems.

On the other hand, the current Harari orthography (fidäl) looks fairly consistent vis-a-vis Amharic orthography, at least in representing consonant sounds. Moreover, it avoids the problem of under-differentiation and over-differentiation, since the Harari orthography has eliminated the extra or redundant graphemes not useful for Harari. However, there are unsettled issues when it comes to the representation of vowel sounds. For instance, the representation of vowel length (present in Harari but not in Amharic) aroused a heated debate when a suggestion was made to adopt an Arabic-type of marking vowel length.

Nevertheless, a positive transfer from Harari to Amharic is evident. Since the graphemes of Harari constitute a subset of the graphemes of Amharic, all the graphemes used to write the Harari language are not only present in Amharic but are also consistent in representing the sounds of both languages so that transferability from Harari (L1) to Amharic (L2) is smooth. This, in turn, facilitates the teaching-learning process as pupils are able to make interlingual identification of similar letters, considerably reducing the amount of time needed to get literate in both languages.

For the success of any orthography, however, ideological and historical factors outweigh the technical aspects discussed afore. As a result, the choice of script is by and large a political decision and is largely determined by political, historical and social factors. Political motivation is the strongest factor influencing the choice of script, since different scripts may convey different notions of national independence or ethnic identity. As an outcome of conscious decisions, different orthographies symbolize different identities and are important in constructing national or group identities. Spolsky (2004, 30) provides examples from the former Soviet Republics, where the Soviet Union induced minority languages to adopt the Cyrillic script. With the disintegration of the Soviet Union, however, Uzbekistan, for instance, adopted the Latin alphabet, evidently as a mark of separate identity. The orthographic reforms of Amharic writing debated upon for half a century, and the efforts made by the former Academy of Ethiopian Languages to revise the Amharic script, were part of an ideological battle within the power structure and the society at large. In this ideological battle the historical factor of preserving the alphabet untouched came out as the winner. On the other hand, the official choice of the Latin alphabet for writing Oromo and other Cushitic languages in the early 1990s, following the fall of the Derg regime was motivated by the political factor of marking separate identity.

Religion is another strong factor in the choice of a script. Ge'ez script is used for a variety of Ethio-Semitic languages (Amharic, Tigrinya and others) particularly in Christian-dominated areas. Similarly, the Arabic script has been in use, either officially or unofficially, among the Muslim communities speaking Amharic, Oromo, Somali and other local languages.

Generally, as part of the corpus planning activity, there are three major orthographic concerns (Bamgbose 1991, 135).

1. Designing new orthographies for hitherto unwritten languages;
2. The need for orthographic reform due to practical problems, such as inconsistency and inaccuracy in the representation of the sounds of a language; and
3. Harmonization of orthographies between different languages using similar orthographies.

The concern of harmonization of orthographies involves more than one language; and in our case it refers to Oromo and English, on the one hand, and to Harari and Amharic on the other. In the former case, as indicated in the preceding discussion, there is a need to bridge between Oromo and English by harmonizing the orthographies. This is closely akin to the concept of transferability of literacy skills between the two languages, Oromo and English, which are introduced simultaneously in grade one. Revision of orthography is very often a sensitive and delicate issue both politically and financially. The same sensitivity holds true for Harari and Amharic, though here the problems are minimal as compared to the case of Oromo and English. Lacking here is also a mechanism for evaluation and re-evaluation, which should be a crucial part of any corpus planning activity.

CHAPTER SEVEN
THE NATURE OF THE CURRICULUM

7.1. Background

Fundamentally, in primary education throughout Ethiopia, whatever the subject and whatever the language of instruction, the curriculum framework is based on pre-existing Amharic originals. All materials are developed first in Amharic and then translated into the other vernaculars, with some modifications in pictures and illustrations to adapt them to local situations and cultural contexts. The materials for the two major languages, Amharic and Oromo, are similar to materials used in other regions, such as Addis Ababa and Oromiya. The major exception to this uniformity is in the teaching of local languages. Here the very nature of the task makes it difficult to imitate Amharic originals.

Most schools in the region get teaching materials from the Harari Education Bureau. However, due to the recent increase in enrolment, in most schools pupils are forced to share one book for two or three. This creates major inconvenience both for the pupils and the teachers as it is very hard to do take-home assignments. Apart from this, there is a shortage of books for the teaching of Amharic and Oromo as well as subjects under aesthetics (music and art). In Dire Teyara, a rural school using Oromo as a MOI, and the Model I urban school, for instance, there is a shortage of books for aesthetics and civic education. These are areas to which the education bureau has not devoted much attention.

In schools where Harari is used as a medium of instruction, there seem to be no problems concerning books. The books are obtained from the Harari Education Bureau and each pupil gets one book. This may be due to the comparatively lower number of pupils in one classroom, which amounts to 36 pupils on average. Rather, the problem these schools face is an almost complete lack of teacher's guides. This is a constant source of trouble both for the teachers and for the pupils. The religious-based school, Aw Abdal, also gets teaching material from the Education Bureau for all subjects but Arabic. For Arabic lessons, the school uses the syllabus of a private school, the Awaliya School, in the capital, Addis Ababa.

In the mainstream schools, such as Yeshimebet, there is no problem concerning teaching materials except for aesthetics subjects. And in the international school, SOS, the books are imported from the U.S.A. Some books, like social studies books, are adapted to fit the local system; but the curriculum as a whole reflects the U.S. system. The subjects under aesthetics are also covered well, in contrast to the lack of teaching materials for aesthetics in other schools. The music class at the SOS, for instance, is fully furnished with musical instruments and music books. The children are well instructed by professional music teachers, who also seem to thoroughly enjoy the lesson. The average number of pupils in one class is not more than 30 and the teachers manage the classroom very comfortably.

Generally, the schools within the region are at very different levels as regards material resources, curriculum development and standardization of the languages being used in the school curriculum. The following section focuses on language teaching materials for grade one, where teaching in the mother tongue begins.

7.2. Preparation, Structure and Content of Language Teaching Materials

There are only minor differences in structure and content between the teaching materials prepared in different vernaculars. Here, we shall consider only the two vernaculars, Harari and Oromo.

The language teaching materials prepared for grade one consist of nine lessons complemented by a teacher's guide. The textbook has 99 pages and the time allocated to teach the nine lessons is 21 sessions. Each lesson has its own objectives. There are ample pictures and illustrations. The total number of words used altogether in the lessons is 442 words and 99 short phrases and sentences. The textbook covers the alphabet (Lesson 3), a lesson for teaching writing (Lesson 4), two lessons for teaching reading skills (Lessons 5 & 6), a lesson for punctuation (Lesson 7), reading passages (Lesson 8), and revisions (Lesson 9). Lesson 2 focuses on norms of greetings. The purpose of Lesson 1, which deals with various sounds of animals, is not clear and seems to be detached from the main purpose of providing basic literacy skills.

7.2.1. The Contents of the Language Teaching Material

Lesson One: 'Sounds of Domestic Animals'

As stated in the teacher's guide, Lesson One has the following objectives: (a) to enable pupils to identify sounds of domestic animals (cow, sheep, donkey, dog), monkey and lion as well as the sounds of birds; and (b) to help the pupils practice the sounds of those animals. The pictures nevertheless include a baby and a man as well. Neither the teaching materials nor the teacher's guide says anything about how to teach the sounds of those animals, or the purpose or objective of teaching animal sounds in a language class on the very first day. We may assume that it could be to entertain or excite pupils on the first day of the class. However, there surely are better ways of doing this—by asking pupils to introduce themselves to each other, or telling them stories, etc.

If the idea is to introduce these animals and their sounds to the pupils, this would seem to be pointless if we consider the age of the pupils, which generally ranges from seven to twelve years, and their background, as they are not urban children. The pupils must be very familiar with most of these animals by that age, from their everyday environment. The main problem with the text in general and this lesson in particular is the fact that it is translated directly from an Amharic-language teaching materials which are evidently oriented to city children.

Lesson Two: 'Dialogues, Conversations and Greetings'

Lesson Two has the following objectives:

a) pupils listen to conversations of people;

b) pupils identify the contents of the conversation; and

c) pupils learn the norms of greetings.

Only two pictures are given in this lesson. The first picture has two girls talking to each other, one with a ball in her hand; the second consists of two elderly people having a conversation.

In addition, the teacher's guide includes a sample of formal greetings between two people. It also asks the teacher to sing a song for the pupils. The teacher's guide further asks the teacher to tell the pupils a story and encourage them to tell stories themselves.

Lesson Three: 'The Alphabet'

Lesson Three introduces the distinctive sounds (phonemes) of the language, given that the pupils are complete beginners. The text gives the orthography, which consists of the phonemes of the language as well as sounds borrowed into the vernacular from or through Amharic. For a detailed discussion of the development of orthographies in the region, see Chapter Six.

Lesson Four: 'Writing Skills'

The purpose of lesson four is to teach pupils the basic skills of writing. The lesson includes both the manual skills needed for writing and the visual skills needed for recognizing letters in reading.

Teaching manual skills, which is a pre-reading stage, involves teaching pupils to hold and use a pencil and to copy shapes. This is done by giving practice in drawing, then having the pupils try to draw specific shapes: stroke, slash, semi-circle, circle, etc. Pupils are then asked to copy the actual shapes of the letters or graphemes. The emphasis is not on writing but simply on learning to draw shapes.

Teaching visual skills means teaching the pupils to differentiate between left and right, to distinguish similar but different shapes, and to recognize shapes that are identical.

Lesson Four is given in six sessions. In teaching the pupils to identify, recognize and write the symbols, different methods are suggested in the teacher's guide, such as using tape-recorded materials, the chart itself and cut-out cartoons in the shape of the symbols. In doing so, pupils are expected to listen to the pronunciation of each sound from the teacher or from a tape for a dictation, learn to identify each symbol with the proper pronunciation and learn how to write each symbol by copying them from the blackboard.

In order to teach writing skills, the Oromo graphemes are arranged into six groups according to similarity of letter shapes as shown here.

1. I   L   E   F   H   T
2. K   W   A   X   Y
3. M   N   U   J
4. C   G   O   Q   S
5. D   P   R   B
6. ☞   CH   PH   SH

For instance, the first group of graphemes involves only horizontal and vertical lines, while the second group also involves diagonal strokes as in 'X' and 'Y'. It is also suggested in the teacher's guide that it is possible, for instance, to regroup Group 1 into three subgroups and teach them accordingly.

1. I   L
2. E   F
3. H   T

For teaching penmanship, a separate workbook containing examples of handwriting and space for practice can be used, but this can be difficult for financial reasons.

The approach followed in teaching how to write is the same as that employed in teaching pre-reading practice, i.e. synthetic approach (see section 7.3.) in which writing starts with letters rather than the whole word.

Lesson Five: 'Sounds and Word Formation'

This lesson covers the largest portion of the pupil text, 54 pages out of the 99 pages. Its main objective is to teach pupils to read and write words and phrases based on the letters they have been introduced to in previous lessons. The lesson basically teaches how to form a word using the phonemes or sounds introduced earlier.

What is actually done and what should be done are typically very different. The list of words to be taught should (but does not) include the different patterns in which the symbols will occur, such as the initial, medial and final parts of words, as well as the common grammatical words of the language. The principle should be to introduce the most frequently used sounds first, since in all languages certain phonemes are used much more frequently than others and these are the ones a reader or a pupil will come across repeatedly in reading. The order of presentation of the sounds can be determined by doing a frequency count, compiling several hundred words of text material and counting the frequency of occurrence of the different sounds. After determining the most frequent sounds of the language, one can plan the optimal order in which they should be taught. When creating teaching materials, it is therefore important to plan the order in which each phoneme will be introduced, gradually, at different points in the lesson. We shall come back to these issues under 7.3.

Lesson Six: 'Gemination and Vowel Length'

This applies to the Oromo language in particular. Examples are given for both consonant gemination and vowel length to show that they cause a meaning difference in the language, and to show how they are represented in writing.

Lesson Seven: 'Punctuation'

This lesson introduces only two punctuation marks: full stop and question mark. The teacher's guide states that at this stage it suffices to introduce only the most basic punctuation marks and postpone the rest for later stages.

Lesson Eight: 'Reading Passages'

The lesson contains seven passages followed by exercises of different formats, such as multiple-choice, fill in the blanks, and comprehension questions. The objectives of this lesson are: to help pupils read the passages and understand the contents, and to encourage them to retell the stories orally in class. Pupils are also encouraged to read in groups or individually.

The contents of the passages are relevant to the cultural background of the children. All the passages are meant to develop the four language skills—listening, writing, reading, and speaking. Thus, pupils are encouraged to listen to the stories, are asked to respond to WH-questions or retell the stories.

The passages are not about difficult or abstruse topics that the pupils could not understand. In some cases, it is the animals that are "speaking". In other cases, the passages talk about the school environment or the coffee ceremony, topics that pupils are familiar with.

Lesson Nine: 'Revisions'

The objective of this lesson is to check how well pupils have internalized the lessons they have been taught. This lesson contains a series of exercises to this effect, which include constructing words from the letters in a box.

7.3. Standardization and Language Development

In this section, some theoretical and practical issues pertaining to the preparation of language teaching materials are considered. Some of the pertinent issues include: How the lessons in language teaching materials should be organized, what the content to be taught is, what should be taught first, how we can determine the order, and what the associated problems of 'transfer' from a mother tongue to the language of wider communication (Amharic) or an international language, such as English are.

The structure and content of the language teaching material for grade one have been outlined under 7.2. In the preparation of a teaching material such as this, there are important issues that need to be considered. These include:

1) selection of a teaching approach;
2) teacher training;
3) bridging between any two languages involved; and
4) other issues.

Selection of a Teaching Approach

There are different approaches employed in the teaching of reading materials for lower grades. These are the Synthetic, Analytic (Global) and Eclectic approaches. The synthetic approach starts with letters or syllables (for the fidäl), which are taught either by name (as in the alphabetic method) or by sound (phonic approach), and then combines them into syllables and words (Neijs 1961, 19–20). One advantage of this approach is that it pays due attention to the mechanical aspects of reading, which can promote accurate recognition of graphemes, particularly as part of word recognition. It is also easy to teach, even by untrained teachers. Among its disadvantages are an over emphasis on mechanical aspects and insufficient attention to meaning, since fluent reading for meaning is retarded by the habit of laboriously spelling out words or syllables.

The analytic or global approach, on the other hand, starts with 'meaningful wholes', such as words, phrases and sentences, which are then broken down into either syllables or letters. The advantage of this approach is that the pupil quickly understands that reading is directly involved with words and meanings since nobody speaks in isolated syllables. As a result, the rhythm and pattern of speech are taught from the very beginning. This approach may better suit the needs of adult learners. Some of the disadvantages of the analytic approach are that it can result in failure to develop accuracy in the visual recognition of letters, and requires relatively highly trained teachers who have to invest a considerable amount of activity and imagination to fully realize the advantages of this approach.

The eclectic approach mixes the synthetic and the analytic methods within every lesson. The advantage of this approach is that very quick progress can be made. The disadvantages are that the rapid changes between synthesis and analysis may confuse pupils and impair retention of knowledge; moreover, the eclectic approach requires a well-trained and committed teacher since the method is labour-intensive for the teacher.

Every approach has its own pros and cons and the choice depends on: (1) the function and purpose of the teaching material, and (2) the nature of the language to be used as a MOI. For instance, the syllable approach, in which the syllable is used as the focal point of departure, is essential if the writing system is a syllabary (like fidäl), and is in general more effective in a language with few or no consonant or vowel clusters. This method would be more useful for languages with monosyllabic words and less so for languages with varying syllable patterns and phonotactics. Oromo has a complex syllable canon and productive consonant clustering. The syllable approach would, therefore, be of little use for teaching Oromo. In fact, the Oromo teaching material utilizes the synthetic approach where letters are introduced first and subsequently key words are built up using the sounds represented by the letters. The analytic approach could likewise be useful for languages with a complex syllable pattern and phonotactics since words are introduced as 'units of thought' irrespective of their complexity of structure. One may perhaps think that the eclectic approach might be the best option to teach literacy skills in Oromo, for instance.

Teacher Training

The Harari region has its own Teacher Training Institute (TTI) in the city of Harar. The success or failure of any basic education programme depends greatly on how well-equipped teachers are in terms of training and provisions of materials. No matter how good an orthography the linguist prepares, no matter how well planned the pedagogic grammar, no matter how good the plans for a pre-reading stage, if the teacher is not properly trained and equipped, the teaching of literacy skills will have very little success.

First and foremost, it is crucial that the teacher be able to read the orthography well and understand the sounds represented by each symbol. The teacher must also be convinced of the value of giving basic education in the vernacular, and s/he must be a good reader. The teacher must understand the methods (if any) that are intended to be used with the teaching materials. If the teacher does not understand how the teaching material works, s/he will not follow the system for which it was designed. It would be unfair to deliver books to a teacher and expect him or her to understand how to use them properly if the teacher has not been trained in how to use the books. Furthermore, many teachers who are not first language speakers of Amharic have received their entire education in their second language, but generally without the benefit of second language teaching methods. They may never have learned to read and write their first language, or they may have learned to write it in a script that is no longer in use. This puts them at a disadvantage when they have to use their first language as medium of instruction.

Secondly, the teacher must be provided with a teacher's guide that explains the orthography, introduces the system used in the book, and explains each lesson. This type of teacher's guide could be an important aid, if designed well. For example, the teacher's guide should explain why the letters are presented in the book in the particular order that actually occurs. It should also explain the use of the Laubach method of using pictures to help the pupil remember the shape and sound of the letter. In short, teacher trainers should take into account the real educational needs and appropriate methods to be used in the schools. If a teacher-in-training is expected to learn new methods and use a new kind of teaching material, he/she must understand how to use it and why it is better than other methods, so that he/she can be comfortable and confident with the new method. Otherwise, he/she will use the old method with which he/she is familiar. For example, if the teacher-in-training has acquired the skill of reading in part by memorizing the Amharic syllabary, i.e. the fidäl chart, he/she may well be inclined to teach by using the same method.

The teacher's guide could be useful for all these purposes. Unfortunately, the reality does not match the ideal. Although teachers are provided with a teacher's guide, the guide does not provide much information on the method to be used, why the letters are taught in a different order as compared to English or Amharic, or the use of the Laubach method in the various lessons, for instance.

These remarks have been made anecdotally on the basis of interviews and observations on the performance of teachers in the six primary schools. Whereas, looking into what the curriculum of TTI consists of and how teachers are equipped in terms of training is beyond the scope of this research.

Bridging Between any Two Languages Involved

In all Ethiopian primary schools, English is taught as a school subject as of grade one. The teaching of English is of particular interest here since both English and Oromo use the Latin alphabet, albeit in different orthographic variations. In the process of designing the orthography of Oromo, the idea of 'bridging' could usefully have been taken into consideration in order to facilitate the acquisition of English as a second language, i.e. to enable pupils to use their literacy skills in Oromo to learn to read English. This, however, was not done.

The concept of 'bridging' is often used to express the idea of transferring literacy skills from one language to another. There are two kinds of bridging. First, if a person speaks two languages and learns to read in one of the languages, he/she can then transfer his/her reading skills to the other language. Second, if a person reads one language, he/she can use this reading ability to help him/her learn to read and speak another new language. In both cases, the person transfers his/her ability to read in one language to another language. Teaching materials should be prepared specifically to help pupils bridge or transfer their reading skills in the sense expressed by Odlin (1989), which involves both negative and positive transfers (see section 2.3).

The potential transfer in the case of Oromo will involve two linguistically unrelated languages—notably transfer between the two languages: Oromo (Cushitic, Afro-Asiatic) and English (Germanic, Indo-European) and between the different varieties of scripts. This may involve both positive and negative transfer features. As shown in Chapter Six, the same symbols (especially "x") can represent different sounds in Oromo and English. In the case of Harari and Amharic, positive transfer is potentially involved: both are Semitic languages, and using the same script (fidäl) will surely be advantageous to the child in transferring literacy skills from the vernacular to the LWC, Amharic.

Other Issues

Other issues also need to be considered, such as variation within the language, the effective use of repetition, testing the orthography and the teaching materials, and follow-up supplementary reading for the pupils.

As regards variation, Oromo and Amharic are well-known for their regional dialect variations and the preparation of any teaching material should take into account the dialect variations that exist within the language. The difference between formal and informal language should also be considered in the preparation of teaching materials. If formal and informal structures both exist in the language, it is best to start with the informal structures, unless there is a sociolinguistic constraint, for they will be better known to the pupils than the formal ones will be. Hence, there is a need to reflect on the patterns of language use in the community at large.

Using repetition wisely in the text is another important aspect of the preparation of teaching materials. Deliberately building repetition into teaching materials is useful for people who are learning to read. This can be done within the context of the lesson, by way of revision or exercises, or by way of summary of content at the end of each lesson. For both Oromo and Harari this has indeed been done for some of the lessons in a limited way.

Testing the orthography and teaching materials is, or should be, another crucial aspect of the preparation before the materials are actually put into use in formal classroom situations, and this should be an integral part of the planning and implementation strategy. The orthography and the teaching materials should be tested, with a small class before being printed or used in the school system. This has hardly been done for any language introduced into the school system throughout the country. Had it been done, it could have allowed syllabus designers to correct some problems in advance. Testing materials can also give a clue as to what should be included in the teacher's guide. If the orthography and teaching materials had been tested, it would have been possible to avoid some of the problems related to transferability of skills. Oromo was the first language to adopt the Latin alphabet when the new language policy was issued by the Transitional Government of Ethiopia in 1991. Many Cushitic languages have simply taken over the Oromo orthography (Qubee), which was designed in a rush without taking into account the necessary linguistic and pedagogical considerations.

Designing orthography and preparing teaching materials cannot be the end of the story. There must be some sort of literature for the pupils for supplemental reading, since pupils must continue to read in their language outside the classroom situation as well. The vocabulary must also be chosen for the basic textbook and the follow-up literature. The compilation of a small trilingual dictionary could contribute a great deal to the success of the teaching-learning process. During the last decade, there has been a steady increase in production of materials in Oromo and to a considerable degree in Harari as well.

7.4. Discussion

One positive aspect of the multilingual education system of Harari region is the very fact that children are being taught in their mother tongue in lower grades, fulfilling what Cummins and Swain (1986, 101) call one of the basic principles of successful multilingual education, i.e. "principle of 'first things first'". This principle advocates that the child's first language has a central role in all aspects of his or her educational, emotional and cognitive development. The giving of basic education in the mother tongue is, therefore, an achievement by itself.

The success or failure of multilingual education depends on several factors. One factor is the intended aim of the multilingual education being launched. Obviously, a clear goal or strategy is indispensable for a successful implementation of the process. Very often, the planning of a multilingual education programme is part of a general social or political policy, and perhaps even secondary to it. Thus, multilingual education is usually not merely a pedagogical strategy to provide basic education but is often connected to other social or political goals (cf. Rubin 1984, 15).

The intended aim of the multilingual education in Harari region, as well as elsewhere in Ethiopia, is thus not merely linguistic but also includes 'semi-linguistic aims'—i.e., a multilingual approach to basic education serves political aims as well. The introduction and use of vernacular languages in basic education as well as in other domains is highly politicized. Mostly the use of local languages as MOI has been based on the political imperative to represent groups of people in the State. In consequence, both Oromo and Harari have been introduced for the purpose of education in the absence of the necessary stages of standardization and development. Particularly lacking are: the selection of an appropriate teaching method reflected in the orthography and the teaching material, 'bridging' between the languages taught in the school system in order to maximize 'transfer', an appropriate fact-finding survey before and after implementation, the necessary evaluation mechanism and the setting of clearer goals and strategies for the multilingual vernacular education.

The use of vernaculars in the classroom cannot by itself guarantee the success of multilingual education. There must be a standardized spelling for the language, and the orthography proposed should be user-friendly and based on a proper linguistic analysis of the sound system of the language. There should also be pedagogical grammars and dictionaries or wordlists available to guide the teachers. If teachers lack proper materials, the potential advantages of switching to the vernacular run the risk of being nullified (Baker 1996; Garcia 1998). Teachers should be trained to teach in the vernacular, and need to be fully cognizant of the pedagogical opportunities teaching in the vernacular provides so that the use of mother tongues as media of instruction can truly bear fruit.

A final pedagogical problem concerns the difference between teaching L1 and teaching L2. The methodological difference involved in teaching L1 vs. L2 has been neglected. For example, Amharic is taught as L2 in the same way it is taught as L1, using the same materials. In Harari region, quite a significant portion of the pupils are learners of Amharic as L2. The teacher training institute must prepare teachers with the relevant methodologies for teaching L1 and L2 in order to ensure appropriate teaching of the LWC. This appears to be one of the weakest points of the multilingual education programme launched in the Harari region, and indeed in the rest of the country as well.

CHAPTER EIGHT
THE POLITICS OF EDUCATIONAL LANGUAGE PLANNING

8.1. Language Planning Models

Educational language planning is part and parcel of the general social and political planning, and is dictated by the ideology of the political system in power. This is so because the choice of language of instruction, for instance, is not only about the pedagogical concerns of the child. It is also about access to a full range of information which ensures participation of citizens; it is also about individual autonomy whereby citizens are provided with a range of options from which to choose; and it is also about 'recognition' referred to as symbolic affirmation of citizens' identities (Smith 2004). These are only some of the political and social goods language may deliver to citizens. As such language has a political nature.

In looking into the ethical dimensions of Ethiopian language policy, Smith (2004), following Pattern (2001), considers three models of language policy: (1) *official multilingualism*, (2) *language rationalization,* and (3) *language maintenance*. The first model, official multilingualism, gives all languages spoken in a given polity equal recognition. The language rationalization model encourages language convergence and highlights the advantages associated with it, such as 'social mobility', 'common identity', and efficiency. This model involves the specification of domains of language use and the stipulation that a certain language be employed within a given context (Laitin 1992, 10). The language maintenance model advocates a principle of 'equality of success', which seeks to make all languages equally successful in their use.

As also indicated in Smith (2004), Ethiopian language policies, past and present, can be described as having the following characteristics: (1) The imperial regime followed a policy of language rationalization through its Amharic-only policy, (2) The Derg regime moved slightly away from the imperial policy by conducting literacy campaigns in 15 languages, but "the centralist bent of the regime and the weaknesses of the literacy campaign itself contributed to a perpetuation of Amharic language dominance at all levels", and (3) The current language policy is a bit complicated when viewed in terms of these three models.

1) There is a clear commitment to supporting and developing even the smaller languages, which looks like the "language maintenance" model. This has affected the mobility of Ethiopian citizens since regional states generally require knowledge of a local language as a prerequisite for employment, elected office or even enrolment for children in the local primary schools;

2) The decision concerning the choice of language for official use falls under the jurisdiction of the regional states, according to the federal arrangement. This policy too follows the "official multilingualism" model since it allows the use of all languages for any purpose. However, it does not guarantee the maintenance of all languages; and

3) At the federal level, particularly in the capital Addis Ababa, the dominant language is Amharic. This is a de facto "linguistic rationalization" model. The linguistic landscape of Addis is entirely dominated by Amharic.

Hence, the language policy under the current government has multiple facets at different levels of the political structure. At a lower level, the ideology of "vernacularization" is dominant while at the regional state level some form of "linguistic pluralism" is the underlying ideology. At the federal level, on the other hand, the ideology pursued is "linguistic assimilation". This multiplicity and asymmetry suggests that the current language policy has an inherent ambivalence that can be described as 'vagueness' and in some cases the policy involves an 'avoidance' strategy. Vagueness of policy formation can be seen at the regional level as regards the way regional governments handle their linguistic and political minorities. There is also an absence of definite implementation procedures. This encourages non-compliance with the rights of linguistic minorities enshrined in the constitution. An avoidance strategy is another feature; this relates to lack of the necessary follow-up measures. The federal government, for instance, is not interested in protecting minorities from the domination of regional governments; good examples are the Kunama and Irob minorities in Tigray regional state (Lanza and Hirut 2004).

As described earlier, the current educational language policy does not neatly fit any of the language policy models. Why is this and what is the underlying ideology guiding the policy both at regional and federal levels? The political philosophy of the regime, as can be derived from the constitution and other relevant documents, is ethnic federalism, which considers language and ethnicity as major parameters in redefining and restructuring the geopolitical units of the country.

The ideology of ethnic federalism was first enacted in the Charter of the Transitional Government in 1991, following the fall of the Derg regime. It was later reinforced by the 1995 constitution that resulted in establishing ethnic-based regional states within the Federal Democratic Republic of Ethiopia (FDRE). Among the ethnic-based regional states that emerged as a result of the redefinition and restructuring of the geopolitical units of the country is the Harari Regional State. The formation of this regional state, as controversial as it may be, has unique features: (1) Its population size is too small (131,139 according to the 1994 population census) to constitute even a zonal administration by the standards of other regional states, and (2) It comprises a multiethnic and multilingual society which includes the

Oromo, Amhara, Harari, Gurage, Tigrawi and other minorities, such as the Somali and Argobba.

The post-1991 political arrangement of ethnic federalism, in its drive to redress the political imbalance of the past and to empower minority groups, has also created new minorities. 'Minority' is here used not necessarily in a numerical sense but in the sense of groups who are vulnerable to discrimination, marginalization and lack of access to political power. The Harari ethnic group, which was formerly a minority, emerged as the dominant power in the newly created geopolitical structure. The non-Harari groups who had long dominated the region's politics (notably Amharas) have now assumed a subordinate political status. These groups encompass largely Amharas, Gurages, Tigrians and Somalis, who numerically outnumber the Harari. The Oromo are officially recognized and share seats in the regional parliament. Despite the demographic imbalance, politically the Harari remain the dominant group and this dominance is claimed to be justified by the principle of 'minority protection'. It is further argued that the constitution of the regional state, which enshrines the dominance of the Harari ethnic group, is considered an 'affirmative constitution' aimed at redressing past inequalities (Yared 2005; Mohammed 1998), a justification that falls short of satisfying its critics (Yared 2005, 2).

The ideology of entitlement in the Harari region is, therefore, based on 'the principle of minority protection' and settlement history or indigenism. The current government has defined the Harari as the indigenous people, and the remainder, with the exception of the Oromo, as immigrants, largely Christian immigrants from the northern and central highlands. The latter are considered as a residual category. They are neither recognized as separate ethnic groups nor categorized according to their ethnic affiliations, because they are considered as belonging to one or the other different ethno-regional states. The principle of minority protection is thus unidirectional; it does not apply to the newly created minorities.

The field of education language planning is a crucial area where the ideology of entitlement comes to the fore as part of the basic linguistic rights of the child. In the region under discussion, local languages, such as Harari and Oromo are promoted to the level of school languages as part of the empowerment of minority groups. Both languages are currently being taught as subjects and also used as media of instruction at the primary level. Interestingly, Amharic has been retained as the official working language of the new regional government and is also recognized as a medium of instruction in some schools at the primary level—a position it has lost in some other regions where it is not the dominant language.

Very often, the planning of multilingual education is not merely a purely pedagogical strategy to provide basic education, but is connected to other social or political goals. As can be inferred from the education reform policy of 1994 that was promulgated by the Federal Ministry, one of the goals of providing multilingual education in Ethiopia concerns the 'rights of nationalities'. In other words, the policy has the aim of empowering minority groups. Empowerment is indeed an important concept in transforming the situation of minority groups and can be furthered by education, particularly by providing quality and equitable education. The issue we are focusing on here is how this intended aim of the policy has been implemented at the regional state level, which controls primary education. Implementation of the decisions of a policy involves planning of some sort. As Bamgbose (1991, 145) rightly points out, any activity designed to effect an agreed-upon policy should properly come within the scope of language planning. This is the topic of the next section.

8.1.1. Language Planning

Bamgbose (1991, 109) describes language planning as the organized pursuit of solutions to perceived language problems. Spolsky (2004, 8) calls it 'language management' and defines it as deliberate intervention to manipulate (modify or influence) language practices. Ferguson (1977), on the other hand, takes a broader view and identifies language planning with the functional allocation of languages in a speech community, such as, for instance, changing the functional value of a language by using it as a medium of instruction in the education system.

There are two levels of activities covered by language planning: (1) *status planning* and (2) *corpus planning* (Fishman 1977; Spolsky 2004). Status planning refers to decisions on the role of a language in a given polity while corpus planning deals with the structural aspects and development of a language. Bamgbose (1991, 109–110) outlines status planning and corpus planning activities as follows: status planning embraces, among other things, "maintenance, expansion or restriction in the range of uses of a language for particular functions" while corpus planning activities "relate to steps taken to ensure that the language itself is modified to conform with the demands made on it by its functions". These activities imply various decisions at different levels of the political structure depending on the socio-political and socio-cultural reality of the country.

In the Ethiopian context, there are two levels of decision-making: the federal government (the higher one) and the other is the regional or zonal or even the lowest-level unit, the district level. The main policy decisions are made at the higher level. For example, Article 5 of the 1995 constitution of Ethiopia states, "All Ethiopian languages shall enjoy equal state recognition", in effect all the 80 or so Ethiopian languages are equally given recognition. Article 39 of the constitution further elaborates, "Every nation, nationality and people in Ethiopia has the right to speak, to write and develop its own language; to express, to develop and to promote its culture; and to preserve its history". The constitution gives every linguistic community the right to use its language for any purpose, to promote its culture and to preserve its history. The higher level, therefore, gives general directives on linguistic rights.

More focused policy decisions related to the general policy on linguistic rights, as regards education, are made by the Federal Ministry of Education. The Ministry outlines the overall strategy concerning the use of languages in education. One of these directives states, "Making the necessary preparation, nations and nationalities can learn in their own language or can choose from among those selected on the basis of national and countrywide distribution". The Federal Ministry is not involved, at least in principle, in the choice of particular languages or scripts to be used by geopolitical units. This choice is made at a lower level (region, zone, or district).

The task of implementing the policy or the language planning activity is thus left to the regions and lower level units. This means that the linguistically recognized regions choose their respective official working languages. There is in effect a hierarchy of official status in the languages of Ethiopia. Amharic is the official language of the federal government. English is recognized as the language of higher education and given as a subject as of grade one in all primary schools of the country. These are the two languages recognized at the federal government level. Then we have the second category of languages recognized as official languages of their respective regions and zones. These include: Amharic, Tigrinya, Oromo, Somali, Wolaytta, Sidama and others.

An interesting question is, how have these regional states acted in the treatment of their own internal linguistic minorities? In fact, irrespective of constitutional provisions, some regional states have pursued discriminatory policies towards their internal minorities. The federal government has been unable or unwilling to protect such minorities against the opposition of the concerned state governments. Among the languages and ethnic groups that have been disadvantaged in this way are the Kunama and Irob in Tigray regional state (Lanza and Hirut 2004), various minority groups within Oromiya region, and multiethnic polities in many parts of the country, particularly in major towns, such as Bonga, Gambella, Jimma, to mention a few. Moreover, even speakers of the major languages may encounter difficulties outside their own homelands. This asymmetry in applying the policy is the result of vagueness of policy or lack of provision at regional state level of adequate facilities for primary level instruction in the mother tongue to children belonging to linguistic minority groups in regions where other languages are dominant. In effect, this is a de facto "language rationalization" model aimed at linguistic convergence under the cover of an "official multilingualism" that advocates linguistic pluralism.

In contrast to some regional states, the Harari region, at least in its educational language policy, has an accommodative pluralist approach towards basic education by virtue of recognizing as many as five languages. This policy pursues an "official multilingualism" model which provides an equitable amount of resources and attention to various linguistic groups. The state provides adequate facilities for instruction in the mother tongue at primary level to children belonging to politically and linguistically minority groups in the region. This success story is unparalleled elsewhere in Ethiopia.

8.1.2. Planning and Implementation Strategies

In the literature, there are various language planning models that have been proposed as general frameworks for describing status planning and corpus planning activities.

Haugen's (1983) language planning model consists of four steps: (1) selection of one of the competing languages; (2) codification of the form (implicitly including script choice); (3) elaboration of function (developing the language for modern use); and (4) acceptance by the community (approval at the societal and community level). Some of these stages may be collapsed into one and form a single step.

In a model developed by Rubin and Jernuud (1971), language planning begins with initial fact-finding (gathering all required information before decisions are to be made) followed by policy formation; policy formulation involves establishing the goal or the intended aim, selection of means and prediction of outcomes. Then comes the implementation phase. The planning process involves evaluation at every stage.

In light of these models, how are the planning and implementation strategies designed and formulated in the Harari region and in Ethiopia in general?

(1) The Requirement of Fact-finding: Under normal circumstances, it would be expected that fact-finding would precede policy decisions and that decisions would be made based on knowledge of all the relevant facts. To the contrary, in many African countries, as Bamgbose (1991, 141) reports, fact-finding takes place after policy decisions are made. The kind of fact-finding that took place in Ethiopia was largely post-policy fact-finding or at best fact-finding after implementation had begun. At the time the educational reform policy was officially issued in 1994, the policy was already in the process of implementation, at least in some regions, such as Tigray and Oromiya. For example, issues, such as script choice had already been decided upon and orthographies prepared. Implementation preceded policy decisions and in some cases implementation preceded fact-finding.

Bamgbose (1991, 142) lists the conditions necessary for language planning activities. First, goals must be established, means selected and outcomes predicted. Second, the planning should be characterized by the formulation and evaluation of alternatives for solving language problems. Third, planning must be future-oriented.

The Ethiopian case is far from fulfilling these conditions, considering the great speed with which the reform was introduced. It was rather a politically motivated decision focused mainly on recognizing the rights of "nationalities" in using their language. Bamgbose (1991, 143) further argues that when such conditions for planning are not met, we should be talking about a 'happening' rather than 'planning' and the right term should be 'language treatment' not 'language planning'. Following Bamgbose, therefore, one could ask whether there ever was any real 'language planning' process in Ethiopia in general and in Harari region in particular. The answer is there has never truly been a concerted language planning process in Ethiopia. In most cases, the implementation phase and the planning stage have preceded official policy decision. This holds true for the previous regimes as well—the imperial and the Derg regimes. Under the monarchy, the constitution of 1944 simply legalized the already dominant position of Amharic. The Derg regime followed the same pattern as regards Amharic, and in the literacy campaigns which it launched, the planning preceded the policy decision. The whole process was called a "campaign", mobilizing the society into direct action in the spirit of socialism with little advance planning activity.

(2) Political Will of the Leadership: The political will to implement the policy has indeed been demonstrated in Harari, as shown by recognizing as many as five languages as media of instruction in primary education. However, it has to be supplemented by appropriate action and follow-up mechanisms to insure the proper implementation of the policy. There must be a willingness to evaluate and re-evaluate the process and revise observed shortcomings accordingly.

(3) Inadequate Language Development (corpus planning): Due to lack of a clear objective and strategy of corpus planning, the development and standardization of the languages used in MTE is becoming a problem. The truly enormous task of designing the appropriate corpus planning activities still awaits the planners and implementing agencies.

(4) Deficits of Language Planning and Implementation Processes: In order to fill the deficit in language planning and implementation processes, an encouraging step has recently been taken by the Harari regional state. The Harari language has been proclaimed as the official language of the Harari region. To put into effect this proclamation, the 'Harari Language Academy' was established in 2005. Located in the compound of the Harari Cultural Bureau, with very limited human power housed in a rundown office, the Academy is trying to get off the ground and realize its responsibilities with high spirit and morale. This is truly a leap forward in putting the language planning and implementation strategy of the region on the right track. On the part of the political structure, it was seen as necessary to establish this Academy because an expert body was needed to develop and standardize the Harari language. It was also considered crucial to have an institution that could devise a way for the languages of the region to function in harmony.

The responsibilities of the Academy, among other things, include promoting the Harari language so that it can serve as a vehicle for the expression of the cultural, political and societal activities of the people, and issuing policies and conducting studies concerning the Harari language.

The Academy's duties and responsibilities as stated in the *Negarit Gazeta* of the regional state include the following:

- prepare standard teaching materials and textbooks for the different schools that use Harari as medium of instruction;
- describe the grammar of the language and set the standard accordingly;
- compile a dictionary;
- recommend policies that could be beneficial to the growth of the language;
- conduct studies and prepare seminars and symposiums concerning the Harari language; and
- develop a harmonious relationship between the Harari language and other languages used in the region.

After a decade of implementing the policy of multilingual vernacular education, the regional government has now realized the need to have an organized professional body to fill the gap between the policy and its implementation. As the saying goes, 'better late than never'.

8.2. Ecology of Language Paradigm

This section looks into the functional relationship between the languages spoken in the region and their cultural and political environment by employing the notion of "language ecology". As discussed in Chapter Two, linguistic ecology has to do with the interactions between a language and its environment. An environment in the context of language is defined here as the society that uses the language as one of its codes. In elaborating this view, Haugen (2001) states that language exists only in the minds of its speakers and it only functions in relating these speakers to one another and to nature, i.e. to their social and natural environment. Part of this ecology, Haugen argues, is psychological: it has to do with the interaction of a given language with other languages in the minds of an individual bilingual. Another part of the ecology is sociological, that is, its interaction with the society in which it functions as a medium of communication.

Any analysis of ecology of language should address the following ecological issues (Haugen 2001, 65):

- the genetic classification of the languages involved,
- the demographic profile of the speakers,
- the domains of language use,
- the attitudes of speakers towards their languages and the nature of bilingualism,
- traditions of writing (if any),
- level of standardization of each language, and

- any institutional support the language(s) enjoy(s).

Haugen (2001) further argues that the analysis of the ecological paradigm requires not only a description of the social and psychological situation of the languages but also the effect of this situation on the languages themselves (p. 63).

The following sub-section presents outline of the ecology of language paradigm in Harari in light of the issues outlined by Haugen (2001), investigation of the functional relationships of the languages within the cultural environment they are operating in, and the implications of the current ecology of language paradigm for language planning and its implementation strategies.

8.2.1. Genetic Classification of Languages

The languages spoken or currently in use in Harari region are: Harari, Oromo, Amharic, English, Arabic, Ge'ez, Somali, Tigrinya, Gurage and Argobba. Except for English, which is a Germanic language, all the languages belong to the Afro-Asiatic phylum which includes the Semitic and Cushitic families of languages. Harari, Amharic, Tigrinya, Argobba and Arabic are Semitic languages, while Oromo and Somali languages are classified under the Cushitic family (Bender, Sydney, and Cowley 1976). Significantly, many of the languages have a close genetic relationship to each other. Harari, Amharic, Tigrinya, Argobba, Gurage and Ge'ez belong to the Ethio-Semitic family. The two Cushitic languages, Oromo and Somali, are genetically very close to each other, both belonging to the Lowland East Cushitic subgroup. More distantly, the Cushitic and Semitic languages (including Arabic) together assume a common ancestry under the Afro-Asiatic super family. Genetically speaking, the only external language in the area is English, which has a different role and function as compared to other languages.

8.2.2. Demographic Profile of the Speakers

The Harari Region, according to the 1994 census, has a total population of 131,139 people with an equal distribution of males and females. Numerically, the Oromo constitute the majority (52.28 per cent) of the population; the Amhara comprise 32.62 per cent; followed by the Harari ethnic group, which represents 7.1 per cent of the total population. Minorities in the region include the Gurage (3.2 per cent), Somali (1.7 per cent) and Tigrawi (1.7 per cent). The rest constitute only 1.4 per cent of the total population of the region. Of the population, 58.2 per cent are urban dwellers whereas 41.8 per cent are rural residents.

Linguistically, 36.97 per cent of the total population speak Amharic as a mother tongue. The overwhelming majority of these (98.41 per cent) live in the city of Harar and 1.58 per cent in the adjoining rural areas. On the other hand, Oromo is spoken as a mother tongue by 49.79 per cent of the total population—17.54 per cent of the urban population and 94.77 per cent of the rural population. The Harari language is spoken by 7.62 per cent of the total population, all of whom are urban dwellers. The remaining Ethiopian languages are used by about 5.5 per cent of the population. Only 0.05 per cent use foreign languages (including Arabic) as a mother tongue.

As regards religion, the majority (60.20 per cent) of the population of the region are Muslims followed by Orthodox Christians (38.09 per cent) and Protestant Christians (0.9 per cent). In the rural areas, the religious composition is overwhelmingly Musilim (98.4 per cent), with Orthodox Christians comprising 1.4 per cent. In urban areas, however, Orthodox Christians are the majority comprising 64.37 per cent while the Muslims constitute 32.82 per cent. The rural vs. urban dichotomy is, therefore, a central one from ethnic, linguistic and religious perspectives.

8.2.3. Domains of Language Use

In multiethnic and multilingual Harari, there are at least 10 languages used at various levels in several domains. The major domains of language use are:

1) In-group communication: The language of each cultural group, used for communication with people of the in-group;

2) Out-group communication: A language used as a lingua franca among various groups for inter-ethnic communication;

3) Languages given as subjects in the school system;

4) Languages used as media of instruction in the school system;

5) A language used for communication involving specialized information such as scientific and technological information;

6) Languages with a religious affiliation and considered as religiously sanctioned;

7) Languages used in mass media, radio and TV programmes; and

8) A language used as official language in government offices.

Among the major languages, Amharic is used in seven of the eight domains listed in Table 8.1. as the language of in-group communication among the Amhara ethnic group, as a lingua franca among the various groups, as a compulsory school subject in all elementary schools, as the medium of instruction in at least five mainstream schools, as a language of prayer and church sermons in religious gatherings and services in various churches (Orthodox, Catholic and Protestant), in the mass media including print media, and as the official working language of the regional government.

The other two major languages of the region, Oromo and Harari, are used in five of the eight domains, namely, for in-group communication, as a school subject, as medium of instruction, for religious services, and in mass media. English is used in four domains, namely as a school subject in all schools as of grade one, as medium of instruction as of grade seven up to tertiary education, as the language of science and technology, and to a limited extent in the mass media.

Another international language, Arabic, assumes a central place in the life of the various communities as the language of the religious teachings of Islam. It is also given as a subject in religious-based schools and is sometimes used as medium of instruction. The majority of the people in the Harari region (60.2 per cent)—both in urban and rural areas— are Muslims, and accordingly they put great emphasis on Quranic literacy in Arabic. They are also proud of the city of Harar as a major centre of Islamic scholarship since the sixteenth century with a remarkable concentration of mosques, shrines and religious schools (Gibb 2004, 1027).

Ge'ez is the classical Ethiopian language, currently used only for liturgical purposes in the Ethiopian Orthodox Church. Though no longer in use as a spoken language, due to its rich philological heritage accumulated over the last 1500 years, it is both historically and religiously an important language. Other minority languages Somali, Tigrinya and Gurage, are used for in-group communication among their speakers. Somali and Tigrinya are also used in the mass media. Argobba, on the other hand, is a language on the verge of extinction in Harari region and is spoken there by only a few hundred speakers. Its speakers are shifting to the major languages of the region.

Hence, all the languages count for individuals who want to play an active role in Harari society, and the language use pattern given earlier in this section shows the full range of language choice available to individuals. The pattern of language use, in turn, shows the language repertoire of an individual, that is, the set of languages that a citizen must know in order to take advantage of a wide range of mobility opportunities in his own region or country (Laitin 1992, 5). The language repertoire, therefore, gives an idea of the overlapping use of languages by the same people in different social contexts, and further suggests that languages allow one to play roles, not merely to convey information (*ibid*).

Table 8.1 Domains of language use in Harari region

Languages of the region	Domains of Language Use							
	In-group communication	Out-group commn.	School subject	Medium of instruction	Science & technology	Religious purposes	Mass media	Official gov't purposes
Harari	X		X	X		X	X	
Oromo	X		X	X		X	X	
Amharic	X	X	X	X		X	X	X
English			X	X	X		X	
Arabic			X	X		X		
Ge'ez[1]						X		
Somali	X						X	
Tigrinya	X						X	
Gurage[2]	X							
Argobba[3]	X							

[1] Ge'ez is a classical language no longer spoken today but with a very rich philological heritage; it is restricted to ecclesiastical use in the Ethiopian Orthodox Church.

[2] Gurage represents a cluster of distinct languages spoken in the central highlands.

[3] Argobba is a language currently on the verge of extinction in the Harari region; its speakers have largely shifted to one or the other major languages of the area, particularly Oromo.

8.2.4. Nature of Bilingualism

As already noted, Harari is a multilingual region. However, the nature of the multilingualism shows a sharp contrast between urban and rural areas. According to CSA (1994), while 42.47 per cent are monolinguals in urban areas; in rural areas 90.64 per cent are monolinguals, most of them in Oromo. Overall, in both urban and rural areas together, more than 62.6 per cent of the population are monolingual; 84 per cent of the Oromos and 54.7 per cent of the Amharas speak no second language. The Harari are the most multilingual of all the major groups; 87 per cent of their total population speak a second language—47 per cent speak Amharic; 32.6 per cent Oromo; 2.7 per cent other Ethiopian languages; and 4.7 per cent speak foreign languages. As shown in the sociolinguistic survey (Chapter 5), out of the sample population 95.9 per cent of the Harari, 47 per cent of the Amhara and 39.4 per cent of the Oromo are bilinguals. Nearly all the Harari respondents stated that they were bilinguals while around half of the Amhara claimed to be bilinguals.

8.2.5. Attitudes of Speakers

A sociolinguistic survey was made to assess the attitudes of pupils, parents and teachers towards their respective languages and the use of these languages in MTE (see Chapter Five). The results of the study showed that generally respondents are positive about their own language. For instance, an overwhelming majority of respondents, 80.8 per cent of pupils, 96.4 per cent of parents, and 73.3 per cent of teachers, support the use of their MT as medium of instruction and are of the opinion that teaching the MT as a subject would be useful in the preservation of the linguistic and cultural heritages of the speakers.

8.2.6. Written Traditions

Harar is endowed with rich traditions of writing, some going back centuries. Among the languages spoken in the region the following have a tradition of writing:

(1) Harari has been a written language since the sixteenth century (originally in Arabic script) and has acquired an impressive philological heritage;

(2) Amharic also has a long tradition of writing and has acquired a highly developed literary tradition over the centuries;

(3) Oromo was reduced to writing fairly recently and is largely an oral language;

(4) Arabic has an extremely rich written tradition and an immense philological heritage;

(5) Ge'ez, a classical language used only for liturgical purposes, has a rich philological heritage;

(6) Tigrinya has a history of writing, especially in Eritrea, and has a literary tradition;

(7) Somali, though a written language for some time particularly in Somalia, has only a relatively recent history of writing in Ethiopia;

(8) Gurage languages have been largely unwritten until very recently, some are still unwritten;

(9) Argobba is an unwritten language, which is on the verge of extinction in Harari region; and

(10) English, as an international language has of course been written for centuries and has an enormous literature.

8.2.7. Level of Standardization

In terms of level of standardization, English, Arabic and Amharic are fairly standardized languages as compared to the other languages of the region. For the rest of the languages standardization lags far behind. Supportive reference works and documentation in the form of dictionaries, grammar books and authoritative texts are not available for the emerging vernaculars.

8.2.8. Institutional Support

Amharic, English and Harari are languages that enjoy substantial institutional support. Amharic, for instance, has had major institutional support since the beginning of the 20th century, especially during Haile Sellassie and Derg regimes. Harari has been officially supported and constitutionally legislated by the regional state as the official language of the state. The Harari Language Academy has been established to provide the necessary technical and professional support to upgrade and standardize the Harari language. English is also recognized by the federal government as the official language of education. Oromo is the official language of the Oromiya regional state and as such has extensive institutional and political support from the regional state.

8.2.9. Typology of Ecological Classification

As aforementioned, the languages spoken in the region supplement each other in terms of domains of language use and are also in competition with each other—at least the major languages compete with each other for social and functional dominance. Hence, the term 'ecology' is metaphorically appropriate. Some, like Harari and Oromo, are 'identity-preserving languages' and are emergent contenders for the status of official languages and dominance in the region. Amharic, the lingua franca, plays the role of a 'linking language' both within Harari and vis-à-vis Ethiopia as a whole. Religious languages, such as Ge'ez and Arabic, too, play a role in defining social groups. Within the ecology of language paradigm, therefore, there is clearly a functional relationship between the languages and an implicit hierarchy in language planning. At the top of the hierarchy are Amharic, the official working language of the regional and federal governments, and

English, which is recognized as the language of higher education and given as a subject as of grade one in all primary schools. The current functional relationship between the languages and the cultural environment seems to be a mutually supportive one and as such may lead to equity in terms of providing basic education to the citizens of the region.

8.2.10. Implications for Language Planning

The Harari region has a truly multilingual vernacular education programme with a strong component of mother tongue education. The policy pursues an 'official multilingualism model' which provides an equitable amount of resources and attention to different linguistic groups. The regional government provides adequate facilities for instruction in the MT at primary level to children belonging to political and linguistic minorities. However, the question is "is this sustainable"? Two factors may challenge the status quo: one political and the other economic.

Politically, there is a mismatch between the educational language policy and the political arrangement within the regional state. The educational language policy recognizes linguistic groups and gives equal attention to all languages—as many as five languages in primary education. Hence, the policy is maximally inclusive in its nature. By contrast, the political arrangement in the region does not recognize the same groups within its polity and is exclusionist by design. For instance, it does recognize the Amharic language as its official language and uses the language as one medium of instruction in primary education, but it ignores the Amharic-speaking people (37 per cent of the total population) in power sharing and excludes them from participation in the police, the judiciary, etc. This marginalization of the major groups from the political platform, therefore, could create tension, result in ecological imbalance, and conceivably lead to future conflict. Conflicts that look like language conflicts on the surface are very often much more about rights, power, and political marginalization.

Economically, the limited resources at the disposal of the regional government, coupled with the latent political tension, may negatively affect the current practice of employing multiple languages and scripts in primary education.

CHAPTER NINE
SUMMARY, CONCLUSIONS AND RECOMMENDATIONS

9.1. Summary and Conclusions

In the preceding chapters, this study has attempted to present a critical appraisal of the implementation of vernacular education in the Harari region. It also examined the challenges of providing primary education in several Ethiopian and international languages, such as Amharic, Oromo, Harari, English and Arabic. Furthermore, the study tried to assess the use of the various languages as media of instruction for primary education in a comparative sense, from both pedagogical and social perspectives.

As background to the study, a historical survey was made to give an overview of the history of educational language policies and their relative strengths and weaknesses as well as their ideological foundations. Historically, Ethiopia can be described as having passed through six different periods of educational language policies: (1) the religious-based traditional formal education, (2) the fairly tolerant pluralist policy of early modern education, (3) the Italian colonial policy of segregation, (4) an autocratic monolingual education policy, (5) the revolutionary Soviet type, and (6) the current multilingual pluralist policy.

In an attempt to assess the implementation of the current policy, a study of the ethnography of selected schools was made. The implementation models adopted in schools in the Harari region were summarized in Table 4.15 of Chapter Four, repeated here in Table 9.1 for convenience.

Table 9.1. Summary of the models adopted in the various schools

Languages	\multicolumn{8}{c}{Level}							
	1	2	3	4	5	6	7	8
Harari	H*	H	H	H	H	H	h/H¹	h/H¹
Oromo	O*	O	O	O	O	O	o/O²	o/O²
Amharic (Type 1)	am	am	am	am	am	am	am/AM³	am/AM³
Amharic (Type 2)			am	am	am	am	am/AM³	am/AM³
Amharic (Type 3)	AM*	AM	AM	AM	AM	AM	Am/AM³	Am/AM³
Amharic (Type 4)	AM	AM	AM	AM	AM	AM	am	Am
English (Type 1)	e	e	e	e	e	e	E	E
English (Type 2)	E*	E	E	E	E	E	E	E
Arabic	ar/A⁴	ar/A⁴	ar/A⁴	ar/A⁴	ar/A⁴	ar/A⁴	ar/A⁴	ar/A⁴

*H, O, AM, and E indicate the level at which Harari, Oromo, Amharic and English, respectively, are used as a medium of instruction and taught as a subject, while the corresponding lowercase letters h, o, am, e and ar stand for the level at which the languages are taught only as a subject.

[1] In grades 7 & 8 music and sport are given in Harari while other subjects are taught in English,

[2] In grades 7 & 8, social studies and civic education are given in Oromo while other subjects are taught in English,

[3] In grades 7 & 8 civic education is taught in Amharic while other subjects are given in English, and

[4] Arabic is used as medium of instruction for religious teaching in all grades.

The following conclusions have been drawn on the implementation of the policy of vernacular education in Harari.

- It is clearly a multilingual education model, involving the use of three languages. Harari and Oromo are local mother tongues (L1) and Amharic is the indigenous LWC (L2). English and Arabic are foreign languages, (L3). This model is in line with UNESCO's recommendation of having three languages (L1, L2 and L3) in multilingual primary education—a recommendation that follows from the position that teaching in the mother tongue is most effective in the academic achievement and cognitive development of the child. The model implemented in Harari has, therefore, a strong component of mother tongue education.
- The model lacks a proper and consolidated policy towards the LWC, i.e. Amharic. The use of Amharic as a medium of instruction and the

time allocation for the teaching of Amharic as a subject shows the highest disparity from school to school. Amharic, besides its political and psychological dominance, has a well developed literature which provides access to a much wider store of knowledge that can be provided by an indigenous language. Pupils who do not go beyond the first cycle will be cut off from the LWC and the accruing benefits that the knowledge of the language may provide. The drop-out rate for the region in the lower grades was between 18 and 23 per cent in the years 2000–2004. Since these children will have left school before mastering the LWC, which is the lingua franca of the region as well as the entire country, it will be very difficult for them to operate in other linguistic environments they are unfamiliar with. The need for the promotion of literacy in the LWC has not been adequately recognized by the political system of the region.

- This raises the question whether the policy is inherently unequal, denying equitable access to and achievement in basic education, and whether it respects the linguistic rights of the child. As rightly pointed out by Skutnabb-Kangas and Phillipson (1995), as much as a child has the right to learn in his/her mother tongue, he/she has the right to learn the official language of the country as a matter of linguistic right.
- In terms of time allocation of each language within the classroom, a wide range of patterns has been observed between schools, even those using the same medium of instruction. The emphasis on one language or the other seems to depend on the interest of a particular school. This lack of consistency in language allocation in classrooms and the consequent disparity of competence in the major languages across pupils is another shortcoming of the implementation model.
- Unlike in any other region, in Harari parents have the option to choose the school of their preference and exercise language rights on behalf of their children while they are minors. This freedom of choice and opportunity has led to the wide range of implementation models presented in this book. It cannot be expected that any single uniform implementation model could lead to satisfactory results in such a diverse multiethnic polity. A microcosm of Ethiopia cannot possibly operate with one uniform implementation model.
- The implementation model favours international languages over the official working language of the region and the country, Amharic. One of the shortcomings of the policy is, therefore, inadequate teaching of Amharic. Given the lack of uniformity in the teaching of the LWC, the policy has no mechanism to ensure that disparities in mastering Amharic will be minimized, let alone eliminated.
- In the area of language development and standardization of the vernaculars in use in the school system, there are persistent issues about which respondents have expressed their opinions. Lack of advance preparation on the part of the schools before the implementation of the policy, and inadequate involvement of the community in decision-making as well as in the implementation of the policy, were concerns

expressed by respondents. These facts have also been observed on the ground and are confirmed by interviews conducted with various stakeholders, such as teachers, school directors, policy-makers, and parents. Among the problems related to the implementation model and cited by the respondents, inconsistencies in the use of the orthography due to lack of standardization, variations in the pronunciation of some words, and lack of proper terminology for certain subjects are the major impediments.

9.2. Recommendations

This study makes the following recommendations and observations on the problems observed in the educational language policy implementation strategies in Harari region, which will hopefully help in improving the quality of the ongoing multilingual vernacular education programme and in ensuring its success.

a) The vernaculars have been introduced into the school system without the required preparation from both linguistic and pedagogical points of view. Both the orthography and the language teaching materials need to be replaced by revised versions. The revision of orthography and/or teaching materials is very often a sensitive and delicate issue both politically and financially. As suggested by Yri (2004, 53) for the Sidama language, initiating the process of revision sooner rather than later will bring the most benefit to future generations of children learning in the MT.

b) In designing the orthography and preparing the teaching materials, the idea of 'bridging' or 'transfer' between two languages that are in use in the region should be considered so as to benefit the learners. Focusing on the similarities of the two alphabets (Oromo and English; Harari and Amharic) would give learners a head start in reading and writing in both languages (Odlin 1989, 36).

c) There is a lack of clear objectives regarding the policy in general and the implementation strategies in particular. The result of this study shows that educational language policy, as part of general social policy, needs to have clear objectives and sound implementation strategies.

d) The implementing bodies and/or by academic institutions involved in training and researching in the area of mother tongue education should aware all stakeholders, pupils, parents, teachers, policy-makers, and the like about the objectives and importance of MTE. .

e) Teacher training must be geared towards improving the capacity of teachers and their awareness in multilingual vernacular education. In order to improve their capacity, in-service programmes, workshops, etc. should be given on a regular basis, since language policy implementation is an ongoing process of evaluation, change and re-evaluation. Teacher training must take into account the difference between teaching L1 and L2 and teachers should be trained specifically for MTE.

f) The major shortcoming of the policy in the Harari region is its lack of a built-in mechanism to evaluate and re-evaluate implementation strategies; this mechanism should therefore be designed.

g) Fact-finding or research must precede policy formulation and implementation, and the policy should be piloted in model schools before implementation.

As Kembo-Sure (2000, 80) points out, multilingual vernacular education must deliver its benefits to the community so that alienation of children from their home culture can be avoided, their skills and knowledge base can be enriched, and they can grow up integrated into the cultural life of the community.

REFERENCES

Abir, M. 1968. *Ethiopia: The era of the princes.* London: Longmans.
Academy of Ethiopian Languages. 1973. (E.C.). Orthographic reform of Amharic syllabary (in Amharic). Unpublished.
Andrzejewski, B.W. 1978. Some observations on the present orthography for Oromo. *Proceedings of the 5th International Conference of Ethiopian Studies,* Nice 19–22 December 1977, edited by Joseph Tubiana, pp.125–132. Rotterdam: A.A. Balkema.
Achaber Gabre Hiot. 1931. *La v/rit/ sur Ethiopie.* Lausanne.
Asante, B. 2005. Harär. In *Encyclopedia Aethiopica,* vol. 2, pp.1012–1013. Wiesbaden: Harrassowitz.
Askale Lemma. 1998. Some points on Oromo Orthography. In Proceedings of the 1st Interdisciplinary Seminar of the Institute of Ethiopian Studies, June 6–7, 1998, Nazareth. Compiled by Research and Publications Committee, pp. 323–337. Institute of Ethiopian Studies, Addis Ababa University: Addis Ababa.
Bahru Zewde. 2002. *Pioneers of change in Ethiopia.* The Reformist Intellectuals of the Early Twentieth Century. Oxford: James Currey.
Baker, C. 1993. *Foundations of bilingual education and bilingualism.* Clevedon: Multilingual Matters.
_____. 1996. *Foundations of bilingual education and bilingualism.* Second edition. Clevedon: Multilingual Matters.
Bamgbose, A. 1991. *Language and the nation*: *The Language Question in Sub-Saharan Africa*, Edinburgh: Edinburgh University Press for the International African Institute.
_____. 1994. Pride and prejudice in multilingualism and development. In *African languages, development and the state,* edited by Fardon, R. and G. Furniss, pp. 33–43. London: Routledge.
Banti, G. 2005. Harari literature and text traditions. A paper presented at the 2nd International Symposium on Ethiopian Philology. Addis Ababa University, Addis Ababa.
Bender, L.M., J.D. Bowen, R. Cooper, and C. Ferguson (eds.). 1976. *Language in Ethiopia.* London: Oxford University Press.
Bender, M. L., W. H. Sydney, and R. Cowley. 1976. The Ethiopian writing system. In *Language in Ethiopia*, edited by Bender, M.L., J.D. Bowen, R. Cooper, and C. Ferguson, pp. 120–29. London: Oxford University Press.
Blair, F. 1990. *Survey on the shoestring: A manual for small-scale language surveys.* Arlington: Summer Institute of Linguistics & The University of Texas at Arlington.
Bloor, T. and Wondwossen Tamirat. 1996. Issues in Ethiopian language policy and education. *Journal of Multilingual and Multilingual Development*, vol. 17, no. 3, 211–236.
Boother, K. and R. Walker. 1977. Mother tongue education in Ethiopia: From policy to implementation. In *Language problems and language planning*, vol. 21, No. 1, pp. 1–19.

Brenzinger, M. 1997. An evaluation account of Ethiopia's new language policy. In *Language choices: Conditions, constraints, and consequences*, edited by Martin, P., pp. 207–221. Amsterdam/Philadeliphia: John Benjamins.
Carmichael, T. 2001. *Approaching Ethiopian history: Addis Ababa and local governance in Harar, 1900 to 1950*. PhD dissertation in history, Michigan State University.
Caulk, R. 1977. Harar town and its neighbours in the nineteenth century. *Journal of African History*, Vol. XVIII, No. 3, 369–386.
_____. 1971. The occupation of Harar: January 1887. *Journal of Ethiopian Studies*, Vol. IX, No. 2, 1–20.
Central Statistics Authority (CSA). 1994. *The 1994 population and housing census of Ethiopia: Results for Harari Region*. Vol. I (Statistical Report) and Vol. II, (Analytical Report). Central Statistics Office: Addis Ababa.
Cobarrubias, J. 1983. Ethical issues in status planning. In *Progress in language planning: International perspectives,* edited by Cobarrubias J. and J. A. Fishman, , 41–85. Berlin & New York: Longman.
Cohen, G. 2000. Identity and opportunity: The implementation of using local languages in the primary education system of the SNNPR, Ethiopia. Unpublished PhD dissertation, SOAS, University of London.
_____. 2005. Mother tongue and other tongue in primary education: Can equity be achieved with the use of different languages? A paper presented at the 7th International Conference on Language and Development, October 26–28, 2005, Organized by the British Council. Addis Ababa, Ethiopia.
Cohen, M. 1915. La naissance d'une litt/rature imprim/e en amharique, *Journal Asiatique*, ccvi.
Cooper, R. 1976. Government language policy. In *Language in Ethiopia*, edited by Bender et al. pp. 187–190.
Cooper, R. 1989. *Language planning and social change*. Cambridge: Cambridge University Press.
Coulmas, F. 1996. *The blackwell encyclopaedia of writing systems*. Malden & Oxford: Blackwell.
Cummins, J. 1979. Linguistic interdependence and the educational development in bilingual children. *Review of Educational Research* 49, 222–251.
Cummins, J. and M. Swain. 1986. *Bilingualism in education*: A*spects of theory, research and practice*. London & New York: Longman.
Daniels, P.T. and W. Bright (eds.). 1996. *The world's writing systems*. New York & Oxford: Oxford University Press.
Daoust, D. 1997. Language planning and language reform. In *The handbook of sociolinguistics*, edited by Florian, C., pp. 436–452. Oxford: Blackwell.
Dyken, J. and Kutsch Lojenga, C. 1993. Word boundaries: Key factors in orthographic development. In *Alphabets of Africa*. Dakar: Summer Institute of Linguistics.
Eastman, C. 1983. *Language planning: An introduction*. Chandler and Sharp.
Fardon, R. and Furniss, G. 1994. *African languages, development and the state*. London: Routledge.
FDRE. 1995. The Constitution of the Federal Democratic Republic of Ethiopia,. Addis Ababa: Berhanena Selam Printing Press.

Fishman, J.A. 1977. The social science perspective. In *Bilingual education: Current perspectives,* edited by Center for Applied Linguistics (ed.). Arlington, VA: CAL.
Gal, S. 1998. Multiplicity and contention among language ideologies: A commentary. In *Language ideologies, practice and theory,* edited by Schieffelin B., K. Woolard, and P. Kroskrity, 1998: 317–331. Oxford: Oxford University Press.
Garcia, O. 1998. Bilingual education. In *The handbook of sociolinguistics,* edited by Coulmas, F., 405–420. Oxford: Blackwell.
Gebre Bizuneh. 2004. Xamt'anga orthography: Its problems and suggested solutions. In Proceedings of the 15th Annual Conference on Language Studies, pp. 32–47. Institute of Language Studies, Addis Ababa University.
Getatchew Haile. 2005. DLING Bulletin. Department of Linguistics, Addis Ababa University. Interview.
Gfeller, E. 1999. Language equality: Multilingual issues in education. Awassa: Unpublished.
_____. 1998. Learning across languages. In *Proceedings of national conference on Bilingual Education,* held in Awassa College of Teacher Education, pp.193–204. Addis Ababa: Institute of Educational Research, Addis Ababa University.
Gibb, C. 2005. Harari ethnography. In *Encyclopedia Aethiopica,* vol. 2, pp.1026–1028. Wiesbaden: Harrassowitz.
Girma Amare. 1963. Government education in Ethiopia. *Ethiopian Observer,* vol. 6, no.4, pp. 335–342. Addis Ababa.
Gudschinsky, S. C. 1957. *Handbook of literacy.* Revised edition. Glendale, California: Summer Institute of Linguistics.
Haile-Gebriel Dagne. 1976. Non-government schools in Ethiopia. In *Language in Ethiopia,* edited by Bender, *et al.,* pp. 339–370.
Hamers, J. and M. H. A. Blanc. 1989. *Bilinguality and bilingualism.* Cambridge: Cambridge University Press.
Hararri Regional Government. [ND]. Harar: Global capital of peace where the old meets the new. Harari Regional Government Office.
Hararri Regional Government Education Bureau. 2005. Report on student populations in the years 2000–2005. Harari.
Harlech-Jones, B. 1997. Looking at means and ends in language policy in Namibia. In *Language choices: Conditions, constraints, and consequences,* edited by Martin, P., pp. 223–253. Amsterdam/Philadelphia: John Benjamins.
Haugen, E. 1971. The ecology of language. *The linguistic reporter supplement* 25, 19–26
_____. 1983. The implementation of corpus planning: Theory and practice. In *Progress in language planning,* edited by J. Cobarrubias and J.A. Fishman, 269–89. Berlin: Mouton.
_____. 2001. The ecology of language. In *The ecolinguistics reader: Language, ecology and environment,* edited by Alwin, F. & Peter Mu↑hlha↑usler, pp. 57–66. London & New York: Continuum.

Hayward, J. R. and Mohammed Hassen. 1981. The Oromo orthography of Shaykh Bakri Sapalo. *Bulletin of the school of oriental and African studies*, vol. 44, pp. 550–566.
Hoben, S. J. 1995. The language of education in Ethiopia: Empowerment or imposition? In New trends in Ethiopian studies, papers of the 12th International Conference of Ethiopian Studies, pp. 182–197.
Imperial Government of Ethiopia (IGE). 1955. Constitution of Ethiopia (Revised). Addis Ababa: IGE.
Italy, Ministero dell' Africa Italiana. 1937. *Scuole elementary per indigeni, II libro delle terza classe*. Florence.
Jebner, U. 1997. Towards a dynamic view of multilingualism. In *Language choices: Conditions, constraints, and consequences*, edited by Martin, P., pp. 17–30. Amsterdam/Philadeliphia: John Benjamins.
Kembo-Sure, E. 2004. Promotion and sustenance of multilingualism: A partnership between the private sector and the government. In *Proceedings of the Second National Symposium on Language Policy Formation*, pp. 75–86. Lilongwe: Centre for Language Studies, University of Malawi.
Kinef-Regb Zelleke. 1982. The Episode of Eyassu Menelik (1896-1935. A paper submitted to *The Seventh International Conference of Ethiopian Studies* held on April 26-29, 1982. Lund University, Sweden. Mimeographed.
Khubchandani, L.M. 1978. Multilingual education in India. In *Case studies in bilingual education*, edited by Spolsky, B. and R.L. Cooper. Rowley, Mass: Newbury House.
Laitin, D. 1992. Language repertoires and state construction. New York: Cambridge University Press.
Lanza, Elizabeth and Hirut Woldemariam. 2004. Language ideology and education in Ethiopia: The role of English and Amharic in Tigray. A paper read at Sociolinguistics Symposium 15.
Leggese Lemma. 1984. Educational transformation in revolutionary Ethiopia. In Proceedings of the 8th International Conference of Ethiopian Studies, Vol. I (A.A.), pp 331–337.
Matheme Sillase Welde Mesqel. 1942. E.C. *Z⟩ krE NEgEr (Memorial) 1949–1950*, Addis Ababa: Nesanet Printing Press. Improved edition, Addis Ababa: Artistic Printing Press, pp. 985 (1962 E.C.) (1970).
Mchazine, H. 2003. Implementing multilingual education in an African setting. In *Implementing multilingual education: Proceedings of the 4th National Symposium on Language Policy and Implementation*, edited by Joachim, F. P. (ed.), pp. 14–25. University of Malawi: Centre for Language Studies.
McNabb, C. 1984. From traditional practice to current policy. In *8th International Conference of Ethiopian Studies*, edited by Taddese Beyene, Vol. I, pp. 715–772.
McNabb, C. 1989. *Language policy and language practice: Implementation dilemmas in Ethiopian education*. Stockholm: Institute of International Education.
Military Government of Revolutionary Ethiopia (MGRE). 1974. Draft Constitution of Ethiopia. MGRE, Addis Ababa: Berhanena Selam Printing Press.

Ministry of Education. 1994. *Education and training policy*. Addis Ababa: Ministry of Education.
Moges Yigezu. 2005. On K'abena orthography. *LISSAN-Journal of African Languages & Linguistics*, Vol. XIX, No. II, pp. 211–231.
Mohammed Tewfik. 1998. Structure, representation and distribution of power as a means of protection of minority rights: The case of Harari constitution. Addis Ababa. Unpublished.
Muhlhausler, P. 1997. Language ecology–contact without conflict. In *Language choices: Conditions, constraints, and consequences*, edited by Martin, P., pp. 3–16. Amsterdam/Philadeliphia: John Benjamins.
Negarit Gazeta. 1944. Regulations on the establishment of missions. Decree No. 3 of 1944, Addis Ababa. Berhanena Selam Printing Press.
Negarit Gazeta. 1972. Establishment of the National Academy of the Amharic Language. Establishement order No. 79 of 1972, Addis Ababa: Berhanena Selam Printing Press.
Neijs, K. 1961. *Literacy primers: Construction, evaluation and use*. Paris: UNESCO.
Ober, H. J. 1965. *Writing: Man's great invention*. Baltimore: The Peabody Institute.
Odlin, T. 1989. *Language transfer: Cross-linguistic influence in language teaching*. Oxford: Oxford University Press.
Pankhurst, R. 1962. The foundations of education, printing, newspapers, book-production, libraries, and literature in Ethiopia, *Ethiopian Obserber*, vi: 241–90.
Pankhurst, R. 1968. *Economic history of Ethiopia, 1800–1935*. Addis Ababa: Haile Sellassie I University Press.
Pankhurst, R. 1976. Historical background of education in Ethiopia. In *Language in Ethiopia*, edited by Bender *et al.,* pp. 305–323. London: Oxford University Press.
Pattern, A. 2001. Political theory and language policy. *Political theory*, vol. 29, No. 5, pp. 691–715.
Pursley, L. 1997. Language in education: The implementation of policy reform in the SNNPR. A paper presented at the Conference on Language Research and Development, April 14–16, 1997, Awassa, Ethiopia.
Rawls, J. 1973. *The theory of justice*. Oxford: Oxford University Press.
Romaine, S. 1994. Language in Society: An Introduction to Sociolinguistics. Oxford: Oxford University Press.
Rosen, E. 1907. *Eine deutsche Gesandtschaft in Abessinien*. Leipzig.
Rubin, J. and B.H. Jernudd. 1971. Can language be planned? Sociolinguisitc theory and practice for developing nations, pp. ix–xi and xiii–xxiv. Honolulu: University of Hawaii.
Rubin, J. 1984. Bilingual education and language planning. In *Language planning and language education,* edited by Chris, K., pp. 4–16. London: George Allen and Unwin.
Ruiz, R. 1984. Orientations in language planning. *NABE Journal* 8(2), 15–34.
Salzmann, Z. 1998. *Language, culture and society: An introduction to linguistic anthropology*. Second edition. Oxford/Colorado: Westview Press.

Schiffman, H.F. 1996. *Linguistic culture and language policy: The politics of language*. London: Routledge.
Selinker, L. 1992. *Rediscovering interlanguage*. London: Longman.
Sergew Hablesellassie. 1969. Amharic as a literary language prior to the 19th century. A paper presented at the Ethiopian Language Conference, Oct. 30–Nov. 1, 1969.
Sharwood Smith, M. 1994. *Second language learning: Theoretical foundations*. London: Longman.
Skutnabb-Kangas, T. 2000. *Linguistic genocide in education–or worldwide diversity and human rights?* Mahwah, New Jersey: Lawrence Erlbaum.
Skutnabb-Kangas, T. and R. Phillipson (eds.). 1995. *Linguistic human rights. Overcoming linguistic discrimination*. Berlin: Mouton de Gruyter.
Smith, L. 2004. The political context of language policy. In Proceedings of the 15th Annual Conference on Language Studies, pp. 6–10. Addis Ababa: Addis Ababa University, Institute of Language Studies.
Spolsky, B. 2004. *Language policy: Key topics in sociolinguistics*. Cambridge: Cambridge University Press.
Srivastava, R.N. 1984 (a). Literacy education for minorities: A case study from India. In *Linguistic minorities and literacy,* edited by Coulmas, F.. Berlin: Mouton de Gruyter.
Srivastava, R.N. 1984 (b). Consequences of initiating literacy in the second language. In *Linguistic minorities and literacy,* edited by Coulmas, F. Berlin: Mouton de Gruyter.
Tekeste Negash. 1990. *The crisis of Ethiopian education: Some implications for nation-building.* Uppsala, Sweden: Department of Education, Uppsala University.
Teshome Wagaw. 1979. *Education in Ethiopia: Prospect and retrospect.* Ann Arbor, MI:University of Michigan Press.
Tosi, A. 1988. The jewel in the crown of modern prince: The new approach to bilingualism in multicultural education in England. In *Minority education: From shame to struggle*, edited by Skutnabb-Kangas, T. and J. Cummins. Clevedon: Multilingual Matters.
Trimingham, J. S. 1976. *Islam in Ethiopia*. London: Frank Cass.
Trueba, H.T. 1991. The role of culture in bilingual instruction. In *Bilingual education: Festschrift in honor of Joshua A. Fishman* (vol. I), edited by Gracia, O. Amsterdam/Philadelphia: John Benjamins.
UNESCO. 2003. Education in a multilingual world. UNESCO Education Position Paper. Paris.
_____. 2002. *Medium-term strategy (2002–2007) for the Africa region*. Dakar, Senegal: UNESCO.
_____. 1953. The use of vernacular languages in education. Monographs on Fundamentals of Education, No. 8. Paris.
Waldron, S.R. 1978. Harar: The Muslim city in Ethiopia. In Proceedings of the Fifth International Conference of Ethiopian Studies, edited by Joseph Tubiana, pp. 239–257. Rotterdam: A.A. Balkema.
Woolard, K. and Schieffelin, R. 1994. Language ideology. *Annual Review of Anthropology* 23, 55–82.

Yared Belete. 2005. The political inclusion and exclusion of Non-Harari ethnic community in the Harari Peoples' State: A case study of ethno-politics management. OSSREA. *Mimeographed*.

Yri, K.M. 2004. Orthography and phonology in Sidaamu Afo (Sidamo). *Journal of Ethiopian Studies*, vol. 35, No. 1, pp. 41–55.

About the Author

Moges Yigezu is an Associate Professor of Linguistics at the Addis Ababa University, Department of Linguistics and Philology, where he teaches phonetics and phonology to graduate students. His research interests include phonetics and phonology of the various Nilo-Saharan and Omotic languages of Ethiopia, mother tongue education, documentary linguistics and sign linguistics. He has published articles in academic journals and contributed book chapters and proceedings articles in these areas. He has also served as the Chair of the Department of Linguistics for several years. Currently he is the Chief Academic Officer for Graduate Program Development and Admissions at Addis Ababa University.